2 Peter and Jude

BHGNT
Baylor Handbook on the Greek New Testament
Martin M. Culy
General Editor

OTHER BOOKS IN THIS SERIES

Luke	Martin M. Culy, Mikeal C. Parsons, and Joshua J. Stigall
Acts	Martin M. Culy and Mikeal C. Parsons
Ephesians	William J. Larkin
1 Peter	Mark Dubis
1, 2, 3 John	Martin M. Culy

2 PETER AND JUDE
A Handbook on the Greek Text

Peter H. Davids

BAYLOR UNIVERSITY PRESS

© 2011 by Baylor University Press
Waco, Texas 76798-7363

All Rights Reserved. No part of this publication may be reproduced, stored in a retrieval system, or transmitted, in any form or by any means, electronic, mechanical, photocopying, recording or otherwise, without the prior permission in writing of Baylor University Press.

Scripture translations are the author's.

Cover Design by Pamela Poll Graphic Design

Library of Congress Cataloging-in-Publication Data

Davids, Peter H.
  2 Peter and Jude : a handbook on the Greek text / Peter H. Davids.
     152 p. cm. -- (Baylor handbook on the Greek New Testament)
  Includes bibliographical references and index.
  ISBN 978-1-60258-313-9 (pbk. : alk. paper)
  1. Bible. N.T. Peter, 2nd--Criticism, Textual. 2. Bible. N.T. Peter, 2nd Greek--Versions. 3. Bible. N.T. Jude--Criticism, Textual. 4. Bible. N.T. Jude Greek--Versions. I. Title. II. Title: Second Peter and Jude. III. Title: Two Peter and Jude.
  BS2795.52.D84 2011
  227'.93046--dc22
                              2010052542

CONTENTS

Series Introduction	vii
Preface	xiii
Abbreviations	xv
Introduction	xvii
Jude	1
Jude 1-2	1
Jude 3-4	3
Jude 5-7	7
Jude 8-10	12
Jude 11-13	16
Jude 14-16	22
Jude 17-19	28
Jude 20-23	31
Jude 24-25	37
2 Peter	41
2 Peter 1:1-2	41
2 Peter 1:3-11	43
2 Peter 1:12-15	52
2 Peter 1:16-21	56

2 Peter 2:1-3	64
2 Peter 2:4-10a	68
2 Peter 2:10b-22	75
2 Peter 3:1-7	92
2 Peter 3:8-9	100
2 Peter 3:10-13	102
2 Peter 3:14-16	107
2 Peter 3:17-18	110
Glossary	113
Bibliography	117
Grammar Index	123
Author Index	129

SERIES INTRODUCTION

The Baylor Handbook on the Greek New Testament (BHGNT) is designed to guide new readers and seasoned scholars alike through the intricacies of the Greek text. Each handbook provides a verse-by-verse treatment of the biblical text. Unlike traditional commentaries, however, the BHGNT makes little attempt to expound on the theological meaning or significance of the document under consideration. Instead, the handbooks serve as "prequels" to commentary proper. They provide readers of the New Testament with a foundational analysis of the Greek text upon which interpretation may then be established. Readers of traditional commentaries are sometimes dismayed by the fact that even those that are labeled "exegetical" or "critical" frequently have little to say about the mechanics of the Greek text and all too often completely ignore the more perplexing grammatical issues. In contrast, the BHGNT offers an accessible and comprehensive, though not exhaustive, treatment of the Greek New Testament, with particular attention given to the grammar of the text. In order to make the handbooks more user-friendly, authors have only selectively interacted with secondary literature. Where there is significant debate on an issue, the handbooks provide a representative sample of scholars espousing each position; when authors adopt a less known stance on the text, they generally list any other scholars who have embraced that position.

The BHGNT, however, is more than a reliable guide to the Greek text of the New Testament. Each author brings unique strengths to the task of preparing the handbook. As a result, students and scholars alike will at times be introduced to ways of looking at the Greek language that they have not encountered before. This feature makes the handbooks valuable not only for intermediate and advanced Greek courses but also for students and scholars who no longer have the luxury of increasing their Greek proficiency within a classroom context. While handbook authors do not consider modern linguistic theory to be a panacea for all questions exegetical, the BHGNT does aim both to help move linguistic insights into the mainstream of New Testament reference works and, at the same time, to help weed out some of the myths about the Greek language that continue to appear in both scholarly and popular treatments of the New Testament.

Using the Baylor Handbook on the Greek New Testament

Each handbook consists of the following features. The introduction draws readers' attention to some of the distinctive features of the biblical text and treats some of the broader issues relating to the text as a whole in a more thorough fashion. In the handbook proper, the biblical text is divided into sections, each of which is introduced with a translation that illustrates how the insights gleaned from the analysis that follows may be expressed in modern English. Following the translation is the heart of the handbook, an extensive analysis of the Greek text. Here, the Greek text of each verse is followed by comments on grammatical, lexical, and text-critical issues. Handbook authors may also make use of other features, such as passage overviews between the translation and notes.

Each page of the handbook includes a header to direct readers to the beginning of the section where the translation is found (left page header) or to identify the range of verses covered on the two facing pages (right hand header). Terminology used in the comments that is potentially unfamiliar is included in a glossary in the back of the handbook and/or cross-referenced with the first occurrence of the expression, where an explanation may be found. Each volume also includes an index that provides a list of grammatical phenomena occurring in the biblical text. This feature provides a valuable resource for students of Greek wanting to study a particular construction more carefully or Greek instructors needing to develop illustrations, exercises, or exams. The handbooks conclude with a bibliography of works cited, providing helpful guidance in identifying resources for further research on the Greek text.

The handbooks assume that users will possess a minimal level of competence with Greek morphology and syntax. Series authors generally utilize traditional labels such as those found in Daniel Wallace's *Greek Grammar Beyond the Basics*. Labels that are drawn from the broader field of modern linguistics are explained at their first occurrence and included in the glossary. Common labels that users may be unfamiliar with are also included in the glossary.

The primary exception to the broad adoption of traditional syntactic labels relates to verb tenses. Most New Testament Greek grammars describe the tense system as being formally fairly simple (only 6 tenses) but functionally complex. The aorist tense, it is frequently said, can function in a wide variety of ways that are associated with labels such as "ingressive," "gnomic," "constative," "epistolary," "proleptic," and so forth. Similar functional complexity is posited for the other tenses. Positing such "functions," however, typically stems not from a careful analysis of Greek syntax but rather from grappling with the challenges of translating Greek verbs into English. When we carefully examine the Greek verb tenses themselves, we find that the tense forms do not themselves denote semantic features such as ingressive, iterative, or conative; they certainly do not emphasize such notions; at best they may allow for ingressive, iterative, or conative translations. Although many of the other traditional labels are susceptible to similar critique, the tense labels have frequently led to exegetical claims that go beyond the syntax, e.g., that a particular aorist verb *emphasizes* the beginning of an action. For this reason, we have chosen not to utilize these labels. Instead, where the context points to an ingressive nuance for the action of the verb, this will be incorporated into the translation.

Deponency

Although series authors will vary in the theoretical approaches they bring to the text, the BHGNT has adopted the same general approach on one important issue: deponency. Traditionally, the label "deponent" has been applied to verbs with middle, passive, or middle/passive morphology that are thought to be "active" in meaning. Introductory grammars tend to put a significant number of middle verbs in the New Testament in this category, despite the fact that some of the standard reference grammars have questioned the validity of the label. Robertson (332), for example, argues that the label "should not be used at all."

In recent years, a number of scholars have taken up Robertson's quiet call to abandon this label. Carl Conrad's posts on the B-Greek Internet discussion list (beginning in 1997) and his subsequent formalization of those concerns in unpublished papers available on his website have helped flesh out the concerns raised by earlier scholars. In a recent article, Jonathan Pennington (61–64) helpfully summarizes the rationale for dispensing with the label, maintaining that widespread use of the term "deponent" stems from two key factors: (1) the tendency to attempt to analyze Greek syntax through reference to English translation—if a workable translation of a middle form appears "active" in English, we conclude that the verb must be active in meaning even though it is middle in form; and (2) the imposition of Latin categories on Greek grammar. Pennington (61) concludes that "most if not all verbs that are considered 'deponent' are in fact truly middle in meaning." The questions that have been raised regarding deponency as a syntactic category, then, are not simply issues that interest a few Greek scholars and linguists but have no bearing on how one understands the text. Rather, if these scholars are correct, the notion of deponency has, at least in some cases, effectively obscured the semantic significance of the middle voice, leading to imprecise readings of the text (see also Bakker and Taylor).

It is not only middle voice verbs, however, that are the focus of attention in this debate. Conrad, Pennington, and others also maintain that deponency is an invalid category for passive verbs that have traditionally been placed in this category. To account for putative passive deponent verbs, these scholars have turned to the evolution of voice morphology in the Greek language. They draw attention to the fact that middle morphology was being replaced by passive morphology (the -θη- morpheme) during the Koine period (see esp. Conrad, 3, 5–6; cf. Pennington, 68; Taylor, 175; Caragounis, 153). Consequently, in the Common Era we find "an increasing number of passive forms without a distinctive passive idea ... replacing older middle forms" (Pennington, 68). This diachronic argument leads Conrad (5) to conclude that the -θη- morpheme should be treated as a middle/passive rather than a passive morpheme. Such arguments have a sound linguistic foundation and raise serious questions about the legitimacy of the notion "passive deponent."

Should, then, the label "deponent" be abandoned altogether? While more research needs to be done to account for middle/passive morphology in Koine Greek fully, the arguments, which are very briefly summarized above, are both compelling and exegetically significant. "The middle voice needs to be understood in its own status and function as indicating that the subject of a verb is the focus of the verb's action or state" (Conrad, 3; cf. Taylor, 174). Consequently, users of the BHGNT will discover that verbs that are typically labeled "deponent," including some with -θη- morphology, tend to be listed as "middle."

In recognizing that so-called deponent verbs should be viewed as true middles, users of the BHGNT should not fall into the trap of concluding that the middle form emphasizes the subject's involvement in the action of the verb. At times, the middle voice appears simply to be a morphological flag indicating that the verb is intransitive. More frequently, the middle morphology tends to be driven by the "middle" semantics of the verb itself. In other words, the middle voice is sometimes used with the verb not in order to place a focus on the subject's involvement in the action but precisely because the sense of the lexical form itself involves subject focus.

It is the hope of Baylor University Press, the series editor, and each of the authors that these handbooks will help advance our understanding of the Greek New Testament, be used to further equip the saints for the work of ministry, and fan into flame a love for the Greek New Testament among a new generation of students and scholars.

Martin M. Culy

PREFACE

When I finished the *The Letters of 2 Peter and Jude* (2006), I did not expect to be writing another work about these letters. After all, I had written about them in *More Hard Sayings of the New Testament*, edited articles about them in the *Dictionary of the Later New Testament and Its Developments*, completed a significant commentary on them, and also published a number of articles that included them. Then Martin Culy asked me to look at the Greek of these two intertwined letters and, perhaps in a weak moment, I could not resist taking yet another look. The issue for me was whether there was anything more to say. On the one hand, my first goal in this volume was to make 2 Peter and Jude readable in Greek for anyone who had mastered the first year of Greek, but then, on the other hand, I realized that the process of closely reading the Greek text brought out rhetorical features, especially stylistic ones, that were not as obvious or, perhaps, were overlooked, in the commentary and other formats in which I have written. In doing this work, I developed a deeper respect for the rhetorical skill of the authors, and I realized that this appreciation was something that one could only get by reading the Greek text. I am thankful for Martin Culy's original offer to me that led to this work and then his careful editing of the work that I produced (and my work certainly needed that editing), and to Baylor University Press for publishing this series, which, is at best a risky publishing venture and thus something of a gift to students of New Testament Greek. And because I could never have written this without my own teachers putting time, energy, and creativity into teaching the language to me, I dedicate this work to my teachers at Wheaton College, the late Dr. Clarence B. Hale, who first introduced me to the language, and Dr. Gerald F. Hawthorne, who helped me to go deeper.

ABBREVIATIONS

1st	first person
2nd	second person
3rd	third person
acc	accusative
act	active
adj	adjective
al	other manuscripts
aor	aorist
ASV	American Standard Version
BDAG	Bauer, Danker, Arndt, Gingrich, *A Greek-English Lexicon of the NT*, 2000
BDF	Blass, Debrunner, Funk, *A Greek Grammar of the NT*
dat	dative
ESV	English Standard Version
fem	feminine
Friberg	Friberg, Friberg, Miller, *Analytical Lexicon of the Greek NT*
fut	future
gen	genitive
impf	imperfect
impv	imperative
ind	indicative
inf	infinitive
Lexham	Lukaszewski, *The Lexham Syntactic Greek NT*
LXX	Septuagint
masc	masculine
mid	middle

MHT	Moulton, Howard, Turner, *A Grammar of NT Greek*, 4 vols.
NA[27]	Nestle-Aland, *Novum Testamentum Graece*, 27th ed.
NASB	New American Standard Bible, 1995 ed.
neut	neuter
NIV	New International Version
NLT	New Living Translation
nom	nominative
NP	noun phrase
NRSV	New Revised Standard Version
NT	New Testament
NTGECM	Aland, *Novum Testamentum Graecum Edition Critica Maior*
opt	optative
OT	Old Testament
pass	passive
pc	a few other manuscripts
pl	plural
pm	a great many other manuscripts
PP	prepositional phrase
pres	present
prf	perfect
ptc	participle
sg	singular
subj	subjunctive
s.v.	under the word (*sub verbo*)
UBS[4]	United Bible Societies, *Greek New Testament*, 4th ed.
voc	vocative
Wallace	Daniel B. Wallace, *Greek Grammar Beyond the Basics*
Zerwick	Max Zerwick and Mary Grosvenor, *A Grammatical Analysis of the Greek New Testament*

INTRODUCTION

This work is intended to be a handbook on the Greek text, so it is a commentary that focuses on the Greek vocabulary and grammar of 2 Peter and Jude. This work is not intended as a full critical commentary on these works. If that were the intention, then this author ought not to have written it, for it would be too close in content to his larger commentary on 2 Peter and Jude (2006). Thus, while that work has been consulted for consistency with this present volume (although one's mind does change over issues over the years), and while there will be some content in this present work designed to help the reader maintain the flow of the text and not get lost in the grammatical details, the comments and the reasoning for the exegetical decisions will be compressed and will focus on Greek terms and structures. The reader is encouraged to consult the earlier work for the more complete exegetical argumentation and pastoral application.

2 Peter and Jude are, in some respects, an "odd couple." They are a couple in that the majority of Jude is included in edited form in 2 Peter 2:1–3:10 (some would put the cutoff at 3:3). This overlap virtually requires that they be read together. They are, however, an "odd couple" in that 2 Peter edits out the more explicit references in Jude to Second Temple Jewish literature (e.g., *1 Enoch* and *Testament of Moses*) yet puts in some explicit references to Greek philosophy and mythology (e.g., the reference to Tartarus in 2:4). Furthermore, while 2 Peter seems to be concerned about a group of teachers who were influenced by Epicurean thought, it is not clear that Jude was writing about teachers at all.

Jude and 2 Peter were coupled in the formation of that collection of works known as the Catholic Epistles. The earliest references in the church fathers to the Catholic Epistles involves a collection of seven works, James, 1-2 Peter, 1-3 John, and Jude. This order, of course, separates Jude from 2 Peter, which depends so much upon it, but it also has the effect of placing a brother of Jesus on either end of the collection as a type of bracket. Furthermore, it includes the three that Paul names as pillars (Gal 2:9) with Jude being included as "the brother of James." (Naturally we are talking about "implied authors" here, or even "reputed authors," for while James, 1-2 Peter, and Jude clearly name their implied author—although the attributions have been disputed over the years—1-3 John simply claim "the elder" as their author, and the issue there is whether that designation does intend to indicate John son of Zebedee or whether it refers to someone else altogether.) Among these works, the one feature that Jude and 2 Peter share in common is late and disputed acceptance into canon lists, with Jude having an easier time of it than 2 Peter. The reasons that Jude was disputed were never stated, but the issue with 2 Peter was its significant difference from 1 Peter in Greek style, tone, and especially use of the Hebrew Scriptures. These would still bother John Calvin in the Reformation period, although, after stating his issues, he basically bows to the decision of the fourth-century church and thus accepts it. In the modern period both have suffered together from a rejection of apocalyptic, while more recently both have profited from renewed interest in apocalyptic as well as in rhetorical analysis.

Jude

Jude is a work that was obviously known and used early in that 2 Peter knew it and incorporated it in edited form into his own work. If it was indeed written by Judah (Judas) the brother of Jesus, then it was written in Palestine (given the strong Hellenistic influence in Palestine, there is nothing in Jude that would make this provenance impossible, and the relatives of Jesus are always located in Galilee or Judea), probably before AD 66 (given that the upheavals of AD 66-70 would have made literary production difficult for some time afterwards), although given that he was a younger brother a later date would not be impossible if he lived to a ripe old age. If it is pseudepigraphical, then one has to ask why it was attributed to Jude "the brother of James" and not to James (who after all had led the Jesus movement in Jerusalem) or some other better-known person.

The work, however, did fall into the category of disputed works later (Eusebius *H.E.* 3.25.3; cf. 2.23.25) and it would be the sixth century before it would be accepted in Syria. We are never told why it was disputed, so any answer to that question is speculative and may reflect the contemporary scholar's view more than that of the ancient followers of Jesus. What is clear is that around the end of the third century it appears both alone ($\mathfrak{P}^{78}$) and in a Catholic Epistles collection ($\mathfrak{P}^{72}$) in papyrus codices and then appears in the great fourth century and later codices (א, A, B). For more on these matters, see Davids (2009) and Landon (1996).

The book itself is in the form of a treatise or sermon with a letter salutation, but not a full letter ending. It is clearly addressed to a known community (since the author intended to write them about another topic before writing this treatise), but there is no indication of where that community is located or how large a community it was. The author shows considerable rhetorical skill in writing to those before whom his treatise was to be performed (documents were written to be read aloud, since most could not read; so one needs to think of the addressees as auditors more than as readers), as is closely examined in the works of Charles and Watson. Jude was not written by an uneducated man or one unskilled in rhetoric. Some of these features will be noted later in the handbook, for they are visible in Greek in a way that they are not in English. The author, however, is writing in a Hellenistic Greek influenced by the Greek translations of the Hebrew Scriptures that he knew, which we usually label the Septuagint (LXX). Thus there are numerous Semitisms in his style, although it would be difficult to argue that he actually knew the Hebrew Scriptures in their original language. The only writing that he actually quotes is *1 Enoch*, and he probably knew that in Greek. He obviously views it as an authoritative and prophetic writing. It would be anachronistic to say that he considered it "canonical," for the canon was still in the process of formation when Jude wrote (see Davids 2009). Thus we can only say for sure that Jude read and was influenced by the Semitized

Greek of the Hebrew Scriptures. A fuller description of Jude's style appears in the work of Nigel Turner (MHT, 4:139–40), although his work precedes contemporary linguistics and rhetorical criticism.

2 Peter

Second Peter is arguably the most disputed work in the New Testament canon, so disputed that for the purposes of this work we can only give a brief overview. It is written in very good Greek that differs from 1 Peter, which is also very good Greek, in that it is written in the more florid "Asiatic" style. It also differs from 1 Peter in its use of Scripture in that, unlike 1 Peter, it does not quote Scripture extensively and appears to refer to the scriptural stories in the form that they appears in Second Temple Jewish literature rather than citing the Scriptures directly (see Davids 2009, 403–16; Davids 2004, 409–31). Furthermore, in the virtues that it promotes and its view of salvation as knowledge it is quite Hellenistic. None of this sounds like the historical Simon Peter. And yet, in 2 Peter 1:1 we find a transliteration of Simeon Peter's name that is only found elsewhere in the NT in Acts 15:14 on the lips of James. The letter also contains an ostensibly autobiographical account of the transfiguration interpreted as the enthronement of Jesus, which might make one think that it must have been written by the historical Simon Peter.

This data is certainly among the reasons why it appears in the lists of disputed works (Eusebius, *H.E.* 3.25.3; cf. 2.23.25), and Jerome (*Illustrious Men* 1) explicitly cites the differences from 1 Peter as the reason its authenticity was rejected. Indeed, even long after its inclusion in canon lists (e.g., Athanasius' fourth century 39th *Festal Letter*) it continued to raise doubts. Calvin, against his personal judgment, only accepted it because it was included in the ancient canon lists, although he did write a commentary on it.

Like Jude, 2 Peter appears in the manuscript tradition as early as $\mathfrak{P}^{72}$ (3rd or 4th cent.) and is found in the great fourth and fifth century codices. In the papyrus tradition, it formed part of "the book of the seven," i.e., the seven Catholic Epistles. It appears to have been accepted first in Egypt and only later in the Western Church, with the Syriac Church not accepting it until the sixth century.

Given the issues noted above, the circumstances of the writing of 2 Peter are naturally disputed. Since the work uses Jude and refers to a letter of Paul having been written to the same addressees, as well as to Paul's having written multiple letters (2 Pet 3:16), it must have been written after these works. If Simon Peter actually wrote it and if he was martyred under Nero (that, of course, is church tradition), then it must have been written before 68 CE, the year of Nero's death. The difficulty with this position (including the fact that 2 Peter knows some type of Pauline collection) has led Richard Bauckham to posit that the work is a testament, a transparently posthumous work, which Bauckham (131-35, 158-62) dates to 80-90 CE. Others date it even later. Likewise, ideas about where it was written (Rome being a common guess due to Peter's association with Rome) and to whom it was addressed vary widely (a church or group of churches in Asia Minor is often posited due to the addressees of 1 Peter, which letter may or may not be referred to in 2 Pet 3:1, and the "Asiatic" style). The addressees, or at least the "false teachers" 2 Peter refers to, do seem impacted by Epicurean thought (note, e.g., the lack of a final judgment or posthumous existence).

As for the Greek style, Nigel Turner has written on 2 Peter as well as Jude (MHT, 4:140-44), noting numerous details about their Greek (some of which will also be noted in the detailed comments below), and correctly seeing the Greek of 2 Peter as relatively rhythmic, influenced by philosophical vocabulary and quite "bombastic," although he wrote far too early to recognize that he is in part describing Asiatic style as opposed to Attic style (with which he often compares 2 Peter negatively); Duane Watson has analyzed the rhetoric of both 2 Peter and Jude according to the teaching of the classical rhetorical handbooks and has discovered that both authors had a solid education; and Thomas J. Kraus has done detailed linguistic work on the letter, similar to the now-dated work that E. A. Abbott (1905, 1906) did on John. Kraus' work is extremely useful, although his final conclusions on the dating of the work extend beyond his evidence. We, however, will see the style better if we examine the Greek text for ourselves.

A HANDBOOK ON THE GREEK TEXT OF 2 PETER AND JUDE

Jude

Jude 1-2

¹Jude, Jesus the Anointed One's slave and James' brother, to those chosen people, who are loved by Father God and kept for the Anointed One Jesus: ²May mercy and peace and love be multiplied to you.

1 Ἰούδας Ἰησοῦ Χριστοῦ δοῦλος, ἀδελφὸς δὲ Ἰακώβου, τοῖς ἐν θεῷ πατρὶ ἠγαπημένοις καὶ Ἰησοῦ Χριστῷ τετηρημένοις κλητοῖς·

The first two verses of Jude are in the form of a typical salutation of a Greek letter. Structurally, the salutaton consists of a nominative phrase identifying the author, a dative phrase identifying the recipients, and a greeting consisting of at least a nominative and a dative. This complex may be long and involved, as in Rom 1:1-7, or quite short, as in Jas 1:1.

Ἰούδας Ἰησοῦ Χριστοῦ δοῦλος, ἀδελφὸς δὲ Ἰακώβου. The author identification is a two-part nominative phrase consisting of a nominative absolute defined through the use of two appositives (δοῦλος and ἀδελφὸς) linked by δὲ.

Ἰούδας. Nominative absolute. The English "Jude" is an alternative form of "Judah" or "Judas."

Ἰησοῦ. Possessive genitive or objective genitive, modifying δοῦλος.

Χριστοῦ. Genitive in apposition to Ἰησοῦ. The meaning of Χριστός as "Anointed One," designating God's anointed king, was probably well-known to the intended readers. "Messiah" would be appropriate if one knew the intended readers were Jews.

δοῦλος. Nominative in apposition to Ἰούδας.

ἀδελφὸς. Nominative in apposition to Ἰούδας. Given the prevalence of Jude as a Jewish name and the fact that Jesus had more than one disciple with this name, the second appositional phrase, ἀδελφὸς ... Ἰακώβου, serves to narrow the referent further, pointing to Jude who is listed as the youngest or second youngest brother of Jesus (Matt 13:55; Mark 6:3).

δὲ. Copulative, but one that indicates that "something new is coming" (Kraus, 167). This puts being James' brother in a different category than being Jesus' slave. The only similar usage is found in Titus 1:1 (see Towner, 666, n. 12).

Ἰακώβου. Genitive of relationship.

τοῖς ἐν θεῷ πατρὶ ἠγαπημένοις καὶ Ἰησοῦ Χριστῷ τετηρημένοις κλητοῖς. The extended dative NP indicates which called or chosen people are being addressed. "People" is implied, since they are the normal addressees of letters; a very few miniscules and the Syriac add ἔθνεσιν ("Gentiles" or "nations") after τοῖς to make this explicit.

τοῖς ... κλητοῖς. Dative of recipient.

ἐν θεῷ πατρί. The use of ἐν plus the dative could mean that they have been loved "in Father God" (NRSV) or "by Father God" (NIV, ESV). However, since the agent of a passive verb is normally expressed by ὑπό, the idea here may be "in the Father," perhaps similar to the Johannine sense of being "in the Father" (e.g., 1 John 2:24). This topic will be picked up again in Jude 21 as a type of *inclusio*.

ἠγαπημένοις. Prf pass ptc masc dat pl ἀγαπάω (attributive). The perfect tense portrays their present state. 𝔐 has ἡγιασμένοις ("have been sanctified"), conforming this to Pauline usage in 1 Cor 1:2.

Ἰησοῦ Χριστῷ. Dative of agency (so NIV) or dative of advantage (so NRSV, ESV). The latter is the more likely meaning: These believers are being guarded (perhaps by the Father) *for* Jesus, so that they remain loyal to Jesus as their ruler. See also above on Χριστοῦ.

τετηρημένοις. Prf pass ptc masc dat pl τηρέω (attributive). The second defining characteristic of these people is that they have been and are being kept or guarded, which is important given the threat that Jude will mention later.

2 ἔλεος ὑμῖν καὶ εἰρήνη καὶ ἀγάπη πληθυνθείη.

The typical Greek greeting was χαίρειν as in Jas 1:1; and Paul normally changes this to χάρις. Jude is using a more elaborate triple greeting that probably developed from the Jewish greeting *shalom* (εἰρήνη), which Paul often combines with χάρις. The preface to the *Martyrdom of Polycarp* (ca. 155 CE) uses a slightly expanded form of the identical formula.

ἔλεος ὑμῖν. The nominative noun indicating the blessing plus the dative indicating the recipient of the blessing was sufficient, the verb being assumed, as in Paul's usage in 1 Cor 1:3: χάρις ὑμῖν καὶ εἰρήνη. Here, there is an explicit verb and the blessing is tripled, using the repeated καί.

ἔλεος . . . καὶ εἰρήνη καὶ ἀγάπη. Nominative subject of πληθυνθείη.

ὑμῖν. Dative indirect object of πληθυνθείη or dative of advantage.

πληθυνθείη. Aor pass opt 3rd sg πληθύνω. The optative is used for a wish or prayer, the aorist viewing it as a whole action. Using an explicit verb, as here, increases the emphatic nature of the blessing over the more typical use of an implied verb ("may X be . . ."). The passive structure, which implies that God will do the multiplying, may indicate a Jewish tendency not to name God in such formulas, although this probably became unreflective normal usage in the Jesus movement.

Jude 3-4

³Loved ones, as I was eagerly preparing to write to you concerning our shared deliverance, it became necessary for me to write to you urging you to struggle for the faith that was committed to the holy people once for all. ⁴For certain people have wormed their way in, who were written about long ago with respect to this condemnation, ungodly people, who pervert our God's favour into sensuality and deny our sole Sovereign and Lord, Jesus the Messiah.

3 Ἀγαπητοί, πᾶσαν σπουδὴν ποιούμενος γράφειν ὑμῖν περὶ τῆς κοινῆς ἡμῶν σωτηρίας ἀνάγκην ἔσχον γράψαι ὑμῖν παρακαλῶν ἐπαγωνίζεσθαι τῇ ἅπαξ παραδοθείσῃ τοῖς ἁγίοις πίστει.

Ἀγαπητοί. The substantival (because of its function in the sentence) vocative adjective serves as a noun of address and here marks the opening of a new section. It will be used similarly in Jude 17 and 20 to mark a new section. The vocabulary links back to ἠγαπημένοις in verse 1 and forward to ἀγάπῃ in verse 21.

πᾶσαν σπουδὴν ποιούμενος. The idiom literally means "making all speed," and it has the sense of eagerness, zeal, diligence, or haste, depending on the context.

πᾶσαν σπουδὴν. Accusative direct object of ποιούμενος.

ποιούμενος. Pres mid ptc masc nom sg ποιέω (temporal or concessive). The present tense portrays the writer in the process of writing when he was interrupted. Thus it means "when," "while," or "as," or, if concessive, "although." $\mathfrak{P}^{72}$ uses the aorist ποιησάμενος.

γράφειν. Pres act inf γράφω (epexegetical). $\mathfrak{P}^{72}$ adds τοῦ before the infinitive, making the epexegetical function of the infinitive more explicit, which was perhaps viewed as stylistically more pleasing.

ὑμῖν. Dative indirect object of γράφειν.

περὶ τῆς κοινῆς ἡμῶν σωτηρίας. Reference. The genitive τῆς σωτηρίας is modified by both ἡμῶν and κοινῆς ("shared/common"). Rhetorically, the use of κοινῆς creates a common ethos and so bonds the readers with the author. It also contrasts with the destruction coming upon the Others.

ἡμῶν. Objective genitive.

ἀνάγκην ἔσχον. This phrase, which expresses necessity, contrasts with πᾶσαν σπουδὴν ποιούμενος, which expresses desire.

ἀνάγκην. Accusative direct object of ἔσχον.

ἔσχον. Aor act ind 1st sg ἔχω.

γράψαι. Aor act inf γράφω (epexegetical). While the infinitive complements ἀνάγκην ἔσχον in terms of sense, and in this sense parallels γράφειν, it is grammatically epexegetical. A few manuscripts (ℵ Ψ 1505) have the present γράφειν, apparently conforming this infinitive to the previous one.

ὑμῖν. Dative indirect object of γράψαι.
παρακαλῶν. Pres act ptc masc nom sg παρακαλέω (purpose).
ἐπαγωνίζεσθαι. Pres mid inf ἐπαγωνίζομαι (indirect discourse).
τῇ ... πίστει. Dative of reference or dative complement of ἐπαγωνίζεσθαι.
ἅπαξ. While this adverb can mean "once" as in the phrase "once a year," in this absolute sense here it means "something done uniquely only once, once for all" (Friberg, 61), as in Heb 9:28.
παραδοθείσῃ. Aor pass ptc fem dat sg παραδίδωμι (attributive). While the verb can mean to hand over in the sense of betray, it often means to hand over, deliver, transmit or pass down (in the sense of tradition), as here. Since this was completed "once" and is viewed externally, and since Jude is not positive about the revisions being made, the aorist tense is quite appropriate.
τοῖς ἁγίοις. Dative indirect object of παραδοθείσῃ. "Holy ones," "sanctified ones," or "saints" are all possible translations.

4 παρεισέδυσαν γάρ τινες ἄνθρωποι, οἱ πάλαι προγεγραμμένοι εἰς τοῦτο τὸ κρίμα, ἀσεβεῖς, τὴν τοῦ θεοῦ ἡμῶν χάριτα μετατιθέντες εἰς ἀσέλγειαν καὶ τὸν μόνον δεσπότην καὶ κύριον ἡμῶν Ἰησοῦν Χριστὸν ἀρνούμενοι.

The reason to contend for their commitment to Jesus as Lord is that certain people have insinuated themselves into the community. These Others (so Reese, 2007) are then described in a summary manner.

παρεισέδυσαν. Aor act ind 3rd pl παρεισδύω. Codex B and C have the second aorist παρεισεδύησαν (cf. BDF §76.2). The verb means "to slip in, worm one's way in, join a group unnoticed."
γάρ. Causal.
τινες ἄνθρωποι. Nominative subject of παρεισέδυσαν. Jude never identifies the people who have slipped in except using the indefinite τὶς plus the equally indefinite ἄνθρωπος.
προγεγραμμένοι. Prf pass ptc masc nom pl προγράφω (attributive). The perfect is frequently used with verbs of writing, for writing produces a "residue" that remains.
πάλαι. The adverb clearly means "in the past" or "long ago," but the author and type of writing are not specified. It can also mean

"all along." Given the temporal adverb, Jude is most likely referring to a Jewish prophecy rather than a heavenly book or an earlier text from the Jesus movement (Davids 2006).

εἰς τοῦτο τὸ κρίμα. Goal (BDAG, 867.1.b). The use of τοῦτο makes the designation of the judgment (or in this case, condemnation) emphatic, pointing forward to what follows (BDF §290.3). 𝔓⁷² removes the τὸ, which in an unaccented manuscript could have been seen as a dittography.

ἀσεβεῖς. Nominative in apposition to τινες ἄνθρωποι. The substantival adjective describes the human beings who have wormed their way in as "impious" or "ungodly." Gentile followers of Jesus were called impious for their neglect of the gods, but Jude is writing to a community that follows Jesus as Lord; so its sense needs to be defined by the following two participial phrases.

τὴν τοῦ θεοῦ ἡμῶν χάριτα εἰς ἀσέλγειαν. They transform God's favor (grace) into sensuality is the first charge. Since it is a transgression against God, they are rightly described as ἀσεβεῖς.

τὴν . . . χάριτα. Accusative direct object of μετατιθέντες. Some scribes (ℵ, C, P, 𝔐) use the alternative accusative singular form χάριν.

τοῦ θεοῦ. Subjective genitive.

ἡμῶν. Genitive of subordination. Rhetorically, τοῦ θεοῦ ἡμῶν ("our God") appears to set the writer and readers off from the Others.

μετατιθέντες. Pres act ptc masc nom pl μετατίθημι (attributive). The verb μετατίθημι means "to transplant, transfer, change or alter." The point is that they are transforming God's gracious favor into some form of sensual indulgence or sensuality. The verb appears in vice catalogues in Gal 5:19 and 1 Pet 4:3, among other places.

εἰς ἀσέλγειαν. When μετατίθημι is used to describe a change of state or condition, what one transforms something "into" is introduced with εἰς.

τὸν μόνον δεσπότην καὶ κύριον. Accusative direct object of ἀρνούμενοι. 𝔐 makes the claim to obedience even stronger: δεσπότην θεὸν καὶ κύριον. While the Emperor claimed the title δεσπότην καὶ κύριον for himself, Jude's μόνον does not countenance that anyone other than Jesus should be acknowledged in this way.

ἡμῶν. Genitive of subordination.

Ἰησοῦν Χριστὸν. Accusative in apposition to τὸν μόνον δεσπότην καὶ κύριον. See also verse 1 on Χριστοῦ.

ἀρνούμενοι. Pres mid ptc masc nom pl ἀρνέομαι (attributive).

Jude 5-7

⁵But I want you to remember—you who (already) know all (of this), that the Lord having at one time delivered the people from the land of Egypt, later destroyed those who were not committed; ⁶and the angels who did not preserve their own dominion but deserted their own dwelling he has imprisoned in gloom with everlasting chains for the Great Day's judgment—⁷how Sodom and Gomorra and the towns around them, which in a similar manner to these (angels) misbehaved sexually and went after foreign flesh, are exhibited as an example, undergoing the penalty of eternal fire.

5 Ὑπομνῆσαι δὲ ὑμᾶς βούλομαι, εἰδότας [ὑμᾶς] πάντα ὅτι [ὁ] κύριος ἅπαξ λαὸν ἐκ γῆς Αἰγύπτου σώσας τὸ δεύτερον τοὺς μὴ πιστεύσαντας ἀπώλεσεν,

Ὑπομνῆσαι δὲ ὑμᾶς βούλομαι. Fleshing out the τοῦτο of verse 4, Jude has three examples of the κρίμα that these Others will undergo. Linking the examples that follow to the initial condemnation (κρίμα) by δὲ (as opposed to καὶ), he thereby advances the argument to its next stage (Runge 2010, 42–52). It was rhetorically proper to assume that the readers were already knowledgeable and only needed to be reminded. That is the rhetorical strategy here as elsewhere in the NT (Rom 15:15; 1 Cor 15:1; 2 Pet 1:12; 3:1). Jude is still addressing his audience (ὑμᾶς), but this is the last time he will directly address them until verse 17.

Ὑπομνῆσαι. Aor act inf ὑπομιμνῄσκω (complementary).

ὑμᾶς. Accusative subject of Ὑπομνῆσαι.

βούλομαι. Pres act ind 1st sg βούλομαι.

εἰδότας. Pres act ptc masc acc pl οἶδα (the perfect form of the obsolete εἴδω). The participle is traditionally read as concessive ("though" or "although"; so NRSV, NLT, ASV, NIV, ESV), but Culy (2003) points out that given its case the participle must be attributive: "I want . . . you who know it all . . ."

[ὑμᾶς]. Accusative in apposition to the earlier ὑμᾶς, stressing that it is they who are well informed. The pronoun, which occurs in ℵ B and 𝔐, is not found in many manuscripts ($\mathfrak{P}^{72}$ A C *al*), and thus could be a dittography, given that the distance between the two occurrences of ὑμᾶς would put them approximately above and below one another in a typical manuscript. However, since ὑμᾶς has been fronted, it would have been quite natural to repeat the pronoun to help clarify what εἰδότας modifies.

πάντα. Accusative direct object of εἰδότας.

ὅτι. Introduces the clausal complement of Ὑπομνῆσαι.

[ὁ] κύριος. Nominative subject of ἀπώλεσεν (and thus also σώσας). The subject is expanded to include θεός in C², Ἰησοῦς in A and B, and θεὸς Χριστός in $\mathfrak{P}^{72c}$. The fact is that κύριος is ambiguous, serving in the LXX as the translation of YHWH. In the NT, it is sometimes used in reference to God the Father, but also serves as the most common way of referring to Jesus. Given that the reference is to an OT event, it is likely that God is the intended referent.

ἅπαξ. The adverb here means "once" rather than "once and for all" (contra BDAG, 97.2).

λαὸν. Accusative direct object of σώσας. Israel is often referred to as "the people" or even "the chosen people," expressions that were later applied to the followers of Jesus (e.g., 1 Pet 2:9, where terminology from LXX Exod 19:5 is applied to Gentile followers of Jesus).

ἐκ γῆς Αἰγύπτου. Separation. No article is used, as is normal with proper names. The same expression occurs in LXX Exod 20:2.

Αἰγύπτου. Epexegetical genitive.

σώσας. Aor act ptc masc nom sg σῴζω (temporal). The aorist is appropriate for a completed event viewed externally and normal in a temporal relationship to an aorist indicative (ἀπώλεσεν).

τὸ δεύτερον τοὺς μὴ πιστεύσαντας ἀπώλεσεν. This is the main point of the clause, i.e., that God destroyed those who did not believe even after rescuing them from Egypt.

τὸ δεύτερον. The accusative neuter form of δεύτερος is used adverbially to refer to "the second time" (BDAG 220.2), or, as Friberg (107) notes, "in a succession of events afterward, later." Friberg's explanation fits the context better than that of BDAG, for the series of events is one of antonyms (save/destroy) rather than two similar events.

τοὺς . . . πιστεύσαντας. Aor act ptc masc acc pl πιστεύω (substantival). "Those who were not committed" or "those who did not trust."

ἀπώλεσεν. Aor act ind 3rd sg ἀπόλλυμι. The main verb is in the final position for emphasis and rhetorical effect.

6 ἀγγέλους τε τοὺς μὴ τηρήσαντας τὴν ἑαυτῶν ἀρχὴν ἀλλὰ ἀπολιπόντας τὸ ἴδιον οἰκητήριον εἰς κρίσιν μεγάλης ἡμέρας δεσμοῖς ἀϊδίοις ὑπὸ ζόφον τετήρηκεν,

At this point Jude brings in a second example of destruction: "fallen angels." While the writer may be alluding to the account in Gen 6:1-4, nothing is said there of the punishment of "the sons of God," nor is it explicitly stated that they were angels (the LXX uses οἱ υἱοὶ τοῦ θεοῦ). Thus, given that Jude will later quote *1 Enoch*, it is likely that he is here referring to the narrative in *1 Enoch* 6–11 (part of *1 Enoch* 1–36, the oldest part of the work, which dates to the third century BCE or earlier).

ἀγγέλους. Accusative direct object of τετήρηκεν. The term can mean messenger or angel (of any type). Here the ἀγγέλους are clearly otherworldly beings, i.e., angels. In the Greek version of *1 Enoch* 6:2, the beings are called οἱ ἄγγελοι υἱοὶ οὐρανοῦ, which adds the interpretive designation of "angel" to Gen 6:2's οἱ υἱοὶ τοῦ θεοῦ, and uses "heaven" as a reverential circumlocution for "God."

τε. This second example is joined to the previous one by τε, which is often used for joining elements of a series. Here, Jude has used τε on its own, i.e., a "τε *solitarium*" (Levinsohn, 106–7).

τηρήσαντας. Aor act ptc masc acc pl τηρέω (attributive).

τὴν . . . ἀρχὴν. Accusative direct object of τηρήσαντας. The expression τὴν ἑαυτῶν ἀρχὴν refers to the "domain, sphere of influence" (BDAG, 138.7) of these angels. This is not the most common meaning of ἀρχή in the NT, but it sometimes carries this sense when used with supernatural beings (Rom 8:38; Eph 1:21).

ἀλλά. The conjunction introduces a contrast that explains what they should have been doing. Indeed, the phrase that follows defines what not guarding or preserving their own dominion or sphere means: They forsook their own dwelling place. First Enoch simply says that they "descended," calling them οἱ καταβάντες.

ἀπολιπόντας. Aor act ptc masc acc pl ἀπολείπω (attributive).

τὸ ἴδιον οἰκητήριον. Accusative direct object of ἀπολιπόντας. The adjective ἴδιος is a stylistic variant of ἑαυτῶν (repetition is not good rhetorical style): "their own" or "what is appropriate to an individual by nature" (Friberg, 202, citing the use in Luke 6:44).

εἰς κρίσιν μεγάλης ἡμέρας δεσμοῖς ἀϊδίοις ὑπὸ ζόφον τετήρηκεν. While this is difficult language, the meaning is clear: They have been imprisoned in uncomfortable conditions awaiting final judgment.

εἰς κρίσιν μεγάλης ἡμέρας. Goal. They are being kept for a particular judgment day; the judgment will take place on the great day. While this expression is rare, it is found in *1 Enoch* 22:11; 84:4. The more usual expression is "the great day of the Lord" or the like (Joel 2:11, 31; Zeph 1:14; Mal 4:5; Acts 2:20; Rev 6:17; 16:8). The referent in both cases is the final judgment day.

δεσμοῖς ἀϊδίοις. Dative of instrument. The term ἀϊδίοις ("everlasting/eternal") occurs elsewhere in the NT only in Rom 1:20, but the expression "everlasting chains" occurs in *1 Enoch* several times. As *1 Enoch* 10:4-6 says, "And secondly the Lord said to Raphael [an archangel], 'Bind Azaz'el [the fallen angel who had taught war and oppression to human beings] hand and foot (and) throw him into the darkness!' And he made a hole in the desert that was in Duda'el and cast him there; ⁵he threw on top of him rugged and sharp rocks. And he covered his face in order that he may not see light; ⁶and in order that he may be sent into the fire on the great day of judgment." While not using the Greek expression, we have here the elements of binding, imprisonment in darkness, and the imprisonment lasting until the final judgment.

ὑπὸ ζόφον. Spatial (lit. "under gloom"). Starting with Homer, this language was used to refer to the gloom of the underworld.

τετήρηκεν. Prf act ind 3rd sg τηρέω. While "keeping/guarding in fetters" is an expression for imprisonment, the Greek reader would not miss the point that the angels did not "keep" their proper domain and so are now "kept" (the perfect expressing the idea of an ongoing imprisonment) bound in the dark netherworld. The word play is deliberate.

7 ὡς Σόδομα καὶ Γόμορρα καὶ αἱ περὶ αὐτὰς πόλεις τὸν ὅμοιον τρόπον τούτοις ἐκπορνεύσασαι καὶ ἀπελθοῦσαι ὀπίσω σαρκὸς ἑτέρας, πρόκεινται δεῖγμα πυρὸς αἰωνίου δίκην ὑπέχουσαι.

ὡς Σόδομα καὶ Γόμορρα καὶ . . . πρόκεινται. This verse continues the main clause (Ὑπομνῆσαι δὲ ὑμᾶς βούλομαι) after the extended participial clause, with the ὡς introducing a clausal complement of Ὑπομνῆσαι (v. 5).

ὡς. Like ὅτι, ὡς may be used to introduce a complement clause (part of the direct object here). It likely, however, places more focus on manner than ὅτι would convey (Culy and Parsons, 212; cf. BDAG, 1105.5; see also Luke 6:4; 8:47; 24:5). Good rhetorical style has variety, thus the τε *solitarium* followed by ὡς, "used to introduce an example or illustration" (Friberg, 416.11).

Σόδομα καὶ Γόμορρα καὶ αἱ . . . πόλεις. Nominative subject of πρόκεινται.

περὶ αὐτὰς. This is good example a PP in attributive position between article and noun, which is good style.

τὸν ὅμοιον τρόπον. Adverbial accusative of manner (cf. BDF §160).

τούτοις. Dative of reference. The antecedent is ἀγγέλους (v. 6).

ἐκπορνεύσασαι. Aor act ptc fem nom pl ἐκπορνεύω (attributive). The participle is feminine because cities are generally feminine and αἱ . . . πόλεις is explicitly feminine. The verb ἐκπορνεύω basically means "to act as a prostitute" or otherwise be sexually immoral, but is used more frequently metaphorically in the LXX (at least 32 of its 47 occurrences) for serving other gods and once for being involved with mediums and wizards (LXX Lev 20:6). It appears only here in the NT.

ἀπελθοῦσαι. Aor act ptc fem nom pl ἀπέρχομαι (attributive).

ὀπίσω σαρκὸς ἑτέρας. "After flesh of a different type." Here, ἕτερος means "other" in the sense of "different" (cf. Bauckham, 54).

πρόκεινται δεῖγμα πυρὸς αἰωνίου δίκην ὑπέχουσαι. The predicate of the sentence is more compact than the subject, but equally complex.

πρόκεινται. Pres mid ind 3rd pl πρόκειμαι. Here, the verb means "to put on public display."

δεῖγμα. Possibly an accusative of content, being cognate in meaning, but not etymology to πρόκεινται (BDF §153). When πρόκειμαι is used in the sense of "to put on public display," what the subject is being displayed as is placed in the accusative case. Here they are displayed as a "proof" or "example."

πυρὸς αἰωνίου. Epexegetical genitive describing δίκην.

δίκην. Accusative direct object of ὑπέχουσαι. Δίκη is the name of the Greek goddess of justice (as in Acts 28:4); as a simple noun the term means "penalty" or "punishment."

ὑπέχουσαι. Pres act ptc fem nom pl ὑπέχω (means). The meaning is "experiencing," "undergoing," or, in a judicial context, "suffering."

Jude 8-10

⁸Likewise, these dreamers actually defile (their) bodies, and even reject lordship and slander glorious ones. ⁹But Michael the Archangel, when he argued about Moses' body as he disputed with the devil, did not dare to impose a judgment of slander, but said, "May the Lord rebuke you." ¹⁰But these (dreamers), slander whatever they do not understand, and, whatever they do apprehend by instinct, like irrational animals, they are ruined by these (very) things.

8 Ὁμοίως μέντοι καὶ οὗτοι ἐνυπνιαζόμενοι σάρκα μὲν μιαίνουσιν κυριότητα δὲ ἀθετοῦσιν δόξας δὲ βλασφημοῦσιν.

Ὁμοίως μέντοι. This phrase shifts the topic from the previous examples to the Others and the woe oracle that starts the next paragraph. The adverb ὁμοίως means "likewise" or "in the same way," and is reinforced by the particle μέντοι (often untranslated, yet serving as an emphatic particle, so in various contexts translated as "indeed," "nevertheless," or, as here, "actually," functioning as an exclamation).

καί. Adverbial: "also."

οὗτοι. Nominative subject of the three verbs μιαίνουσιν...ἀθετοῦσιν...βλασφημοῦσιν. $\mathfrak{P}^{78}$ misreads the emphasis by changing οὗτοι to the less emphatic αὐτοί.

ἐνυπνιαζόμενοι. Pres pass ptc masc nom pl ἐνυπνιάζομαι (attributive). Lit. "these who dream."

σάρκα. Accusative direct object of μιαίνουσιν.

μὲν...δὲ...δὲ. Particles coordinating the three charges (one of many triplets in Jude), the μέν pointing forward and thus leaving one in anticipation of the succeeding δέ (Runge 2010, 93–104).

μιαίνουσιν. Pres act ind 3rd pl μιαίνω. This verb, meaning "defile" or "stain," is always used in a literal or metaphorical cultic sense in the NT, e.g., John 18:28; Titus 1:15; Heb 12:15. Here, it describes the first of the two things that the Others do like the angels and like the people of Sodom. Not only (μέν) do they stain or defile the flesh (which could refer to their own human flesh or also include the flesh of other beings that are involved)—this is on a physical plane—but they also (δέ), like the corrupted angels and others who were mentioned previously, do things on what we might term a spiritual plane.

κυριότητα. Accusative direct object of ἀθετοῦσιν. If κυριότητα were plural (as it is in ℵ), then it would conform to Pauline usage in Eph 1:21 and Col 1:16, and indicate angelic powers. The manuscript evidence, however, favors the singular. Thus, Bauckham (56) is probably right when he argues that it is the lordship of Jesus or God that is being set aside or rejected.

ἀθετοῦσιν. Pres act ind 3rd pl ἀθετέω. The word means "set aside" or "reject."

δόξας. Accusative direct object of βλασφημοῦσιν. The term is unusual, but the evidence of the LXX and Second Temple literature, including the Dead Sea Scrolls, indicates that these "glorious ones" are probably angels (see also Bauckham, 57). $\mathfrak{P}^{78}$ and some versions make this singular and thus parallel to "lordship."

βλασφημοῦσιν. Pres act ind 3rd pl βλασφημέω.

9 ὁ δὲ Μιχαὴλ ὁ ἀρχάγγελος, ὅτε τῷ διαβόλῳ διακρινόμενος διελέγετο περὶ τοῦ Μωϋσέως σώματος, οὐκ ἐτόλμησεν κρίσιν ἐπενεγκεῖν βλασφημίας ἀλλὰ εἶπεν, Ἐπιτιμήσαι σοι κύριος.

We now get a contrasting argument. They slander the holy angels, while the holy angel Michael will not even judge the devil himself a slanderer, but leaves all judgment to God. Thus they slander what they do not understand, while the one who understands all too well leaves judgment to his Lord.

ὁ ... Μιχαὴλ. Nominative subject of ἐτόλμησεν ... ἀλλὰ εἶπεν. Μιχαὴλ is indeclinable, but the article indicates it is the nominative subject.

δὲ. The conjunction here is disjunctive. Codex B has ὅτε for Ὁ δὲ, which is understandable in an uncial with no separation between words and given the fact that manuscripts were often copied as someone read from the exemplar manuscript aloud.

ὁ ἀρχάγγελος. Nominative in apposition to ὁ ... Μιχαὴλ, identifying Michael's rank. While Michael is mentioned in Daniel (10:13, 21; 12:1), the title "archangel" is how he is described in *1 Enoch* (e.g., 20:5; 40:9), where he is one of the four or seven chief angels.

ὅτε. Adverb. "Marker of a point of time that coincides with another point of time, anticipating a correlative, *at one point, on one occasion*" (BDAG, 731). The occasion in view was narrated in the *Testament of Moses*.

τῷ διαβόλῳ. Dative of disadvantage, modifying διακρινόμενος. The adjective διάβολος means "slanderous," as in 2 Tim 3:3. It is used substantivally 22 times in later post-exilic books of the LXX such as Esther, Job, 1 Chronicles, and Zecharaiah to refer to "the slanderous one" (BDAG, 226). Here, the referent of the substantival form is clearly "the devil."

διακρινόμενος. Pres mid ptc masc nom sg διακρίνω. The participle of attendant circumstance modifies the verb of the temporal clause and indicates the general circumstances under which the dispute took place.

διελέγετο. Impf mid ind 3rd sg διαλέγομαι. The imperfect gives the sense of an ongoing argument with its back and forth.

ἐτόλμησεν. Aor act ind 3rd sg τολμάω.
κρίσιν. Accusative direct object of ἐπενεγκεῖν.
ἐπενεγκεῖν. Aor act inf ἐπιφέρω (complementary; BDF §392). In judicial contexts (which includes all instances in the NT) the verb means to inflict punishment or to impose or pronounce a judgment.
βλασφημίας. Epexegetical genitive, describing what the accused is guilty of, and placed at the end of the clause, with the noun it modifies (κρίσιν) fronted for emphasis.
ἀλλὰ. The adversative conjunction introduces a clause that runs counter expectation. Thus this contrasts Michael's actual behavior with the expected κρίσιν mentioned in the previoius clause.
εἶπεν. Aor act ind 3rd sg λέγω. The form comes from the obsolete verb εἴρω. Here, it introduces a direct quotation.
ἐπιτιμήσαι. Aor act opt 3rd sg ἐπιτιμάω. This is the optative proper, used for an attainable wish or imprecation (BDF §384). Thus, either "The Lord rebuke/judge you" or "May the Lord rebuke/judge you" would be proper translations.
σοι. Dative direct object of ἐπιτιμήσαι.
κύριος. Nominative subject of ἐπιτιμήσαι.

10 οὗτοι δὲ ὅσα μὲν οὐκ οἴδασιν βλασφημοῦσιν, ὅσα δὲ φυσικῶς ὡς τὰ ἄλογα ζῷα ἐπίστανται, ἐν τούτοις φθείρονται.

οὗτοι. The resumptive demonstrative pronoun οὗτοι serves as the nominative subject of βλασφημοῦσιν and is emphatic: "but *these*" (BDF §290.1; BDAG, 740), contrasting the Others to Michael.
ὅσα μὲν οὐκ οἴδασιν. This clause serves as the direct object of βλασφημοῦσιν.
ὅσα. The correlative adjective ὅσος (BDAG, 729) is the accusative direct object of οἴδασιν: "whatever things." Lit. "*as many things as* they do not understand."
μὲν. The particle μὲν points forward from their not understanding to what they do instinctively understand, i.e., apprehend: μὲν ... δὲ.
οἴδασιν. Prf act ind 3rd pl οἶδα. οἶδα is "the perfect of the obsolete εἴδω used as the present" (Friberg, 277), although as Porter

(39–40) indicates, it would be more accurate to say that the perfect is used "to depict the action as reflecting a given (often complex) state of affairs" and thus in the case of our verb " 'I know' or 'I am in a knowledgeable state,' " which is why it always occurs in the perfect. The verb has a range of meanings (BDAG, 693–94), but here, as in Mark 4:13, "understand" or "comprehend" is intended.

βλασφημοῦσιν. Pres act ind 3rd pl βλασφημέω.

ὅσα ... ἐπίστανται. This clause is an example of left-dislocation, i.e., the topic of what follows is stated first and then picked up with a resumptive pronoun (τούτοις).

ὅσα. Accusative direct object of ἐπίστανται.

φυσικῶς. The adverb means "by instinct" or "naturally" (BDAG, 1069). It appears only here in the NT, though 2 Pet 2:12 uses the related adjective.

ὡς τὰ ἄλογα ζῷα. Nominative subject of an implied ἐπίστανται. The adjective ἄλογα (picked up in 2 Pet 2:12, but otherwise in the NT only in Acts 25:27; see BDAG, 48) indicates the lack of the reason or rationality that separates the animal from the human (e.g., Philo, *Leg.* 3.30, uses the same expression contrasting animals to human beings).

ἐπίστανται. Pres mid ind 3rd pl ἐπίσταμαι. The implied subject is οὗτοι. The verb means to "comprehend" or "understand." In Mark 14:68 it is used together with οἶδα, while the parallel in Matt 26:70, where only οἶδα is used, suggests that Matthew (assuming that he is using and editing the Markan text) viewed the two verbs as synonyms.

ἐν τούτοις. Instrumental (BDF §195). The neuter demonstrative pronoun refers back to the ὅσα clause.

φθείρονται. Pres pass ind 3rd pl φθείρω. The verb can mean either "corrupted, ruined" or "destroyed" (BDAG, 1052.2-3).

Jude 11-13

¹¹Woe to them, because they have followed Cain's way and plunged into Balaam's error for gain and they perish in Korah's rebellion. ¹²These are the ones who feast together with you, reefs in your love-feasts, fearlessly shepherding (only) themselves. (They are) clouds without water carried about by the winds, bare

unfruitful trees that are twice dead, uprooted. ¹³[They are] stormy sea waves foaming up their own shame, wandering planets, for whom darkness's gloom is kept forever.

11 οὐαὶ αὐτοῖς, ὅτι τῇ ὁδῷ τοῦ Κάϊν ἐπορεύθησαν καὶ τῇ πλάνῃ τοῦ Βαλαὰμ μισθοῦ ἐξεχύθησαν καὶ τῇ ἀντιλογίᾳ τοῦ Κόρε ἀπώλοντο.

The woe oracle includes an implied "to be" verb—"woe *is* theirs" or "woe *will be* theirs"—and is followed by a ὅτι clause that introduces the reasons or grounds for the woe. The whole construction functions virtually like a court indictment. This is one form of OT woe oracles (also found on the lips of Jesus, e.g., Matt 11:21; 18:7; 8 times in Matt 23). The three negative comparisons (each introduced by a dative for what was done followed by the example person in the genitive) increase in intensity from way to error to rebellion and from go to rush to perish. All have in common that in Second Temple Jewish tradition they taught evil to others and they were punished, Cain by banishment, Balaam by being killed by Israel (Num 31:8), and Korah by divine judgment (Num 16:31-35). These are joined in a paratactic construction by καί for rhetorical effect (cf. similar formulas in Num 21:29; Isa 3:9, 11; 45:9-10; Jer 4:13, 31; 10:19; Matt 23:13, 15, 23).

οὐαί. As in Luke 6:24, this interjection is not "a curse but a strong expression for a misfortune, or a lamentation" (Bovon, 225), and in an eschatological context introduces "an expression of pity for those who stand under divine judgment" (Marshall, 255).

αὐτοῖς. Dative of disadvantage ("Woe be to them") or dative of possession ("Woe is theirs").

ὅτι. Introduces a causal clause.

τῇ ὁδῷ τοῦ Κάϊν ἐπορεύθησαν. This is a Semitism (lit. "go in the way of Cain"; see, e.g., Ezek 23:31) for following the lifestyle of someone (often "the Lord").

τῇ ὁδῷ τοῦ Κάϊν. Dative of location with the verb ἐπορεύθησαν, but given that it is a Semitic idiom, the syntactic label does not entirely fit. Cain was known for teaching vice to others (see, e.g., Josephus, *Ant.* 1.52-62).

ἐπορεύθησαν. Aor mid ind 3rd pl πορεύομαι.

τῇ πλάνῃ ... ἐξεχύθησαν. This expression appears to build on the more common idiom above and expresses a greater degree of eagerness to make a poor choice.

τῇ πλάνῃ τοῦ Βαλαάμ. Dative of location with the verb ἐξεχύθησαν, but, as noted above, this is built on a Semitic idiom and thus the syntactic label is again less helpful. The "way" is intensified to the more negative "error." 𝔓⁷² makes the mistake of writing Βαλαακ for Βαλαάμ, both being indeclinable.

μισθοῦ. Genitive of content or perhaps an epexegetical genitive (cf. BDF §167) modifying πλάνῃ.

ἐξεχύθησαν. Aor pass ind 3rd pl ἐκχέω. This is the classical form, but there was also the Hellenistic form ἐκχύν(ν)ω, which explains the form of the aorist passive (BDF §73). The basic meaning is "to pour out" and thus metaphorically "to devote oneself to," or "to plunge into."

καὶ τῇ ἀντιλογίᾳ τοῦ Κόρε ἀπώλοντο. Culturally, of course, in the Near Eastern world contradicting the leader and/or questioning his legitimacy was considered rebellion, not just in Numbers, but right up through the Ottoman period. This expression like the previous one is built on the Semitic idom "to go in the way of someone."

τῇ ἀντιλογίᾳ τοῦ Κόρε. Dative of location with the verb ἀπώλοντο, again with the proviso that the syntactic label is less functional in an idiomatic expression. In context, Korah's "speaking against," "contradiction," "dispute," or "controversy" refers to more than an argument (Num 16:1-3, 11, 12-14) and thus the translation "rebellion."

ἀπώλοντο. Aor mid ind 3rd pl ἀπόλλυμι. The verb means "to ruin" or "destroy," and in the middle voice means "be ruined," "perish," "lose one's life" (BDAG, 115-16). Here, one has what in Hebrew would be called a "prophetic perfect," in which the destruction of the Others is viewed as a *fait accompli*.

12 οὗτοί εἰσιν οἱ ἐν ταῖς ἀγάπαις ὑμῶν σπιλάδες συνευωχούμενοι ἀφόβως, ἑαυτοὺς ποιμαίνοντες, νεφέλαι ἄνυδροι ὑπὸ ἀνέμων παραφερόμεναι, δένδρα φθινοπωρινὰ ἄκαρπα δὶς ἀποθανόντα ἐκριζωθέντα,

The structure here is difficult to follow, perhaps because of the intensity of the denunciation, as will be evident from the changes in various codices. There are two substantival participles (συνευωχούμενοι and ποιμαίνοντες), the first serving as a predicate nominative and the second in apposition to it, with four nominal appositives that follow them. This and the following verse need to be read aloud in Greek to appreciate the rhetorical effect of the repeated sounds that builds toward the end of verse 12 and continues into verse 13.

οὗτοί. Nominative subject of εἰσιν. The demonstrative pronoun emphatically refers back to the Others (αὐτοῖς of v. 11).

εἰσιν. Pres act ind 3rd pl εἰμί.

ἐν ταῖς ἀγάπαις. Locative. While ἀγάπη is common, this plural use for "a common meal eaten by early Christians in connection with their worship, for the purpose of fostering and expressing mutual affection and concern, *fellowship meal, a love-feast*" (BDAG, 7.2) is found only here in the NT. It is changed in Codex A and C^{vid} to "in your/their deceptions" (ἀπάταις) due to some combination of: (1) the influence of 2 Pet 2:13; (2) the Lord's Supper not being referred to as a love-feast in later centuries; and/or (3) the difficulty of accepting that such people were part of these celebrations leading to either an intentional change or to an unintentional mishearing of the word (since they differ by a single letter).

ὑμῶν. Possessive genitive.

σπιλάδες. Either a predicate nominative or a nominative in apposition to the substantival participial συνευωχούμενοι. The masculine article οἱ would at first glance indicate that this feminine noun is not a predicate nominative, but Wallace (331) may well be correct that this a clear example of a *constructio ad sensum*, the masculine article being used despite the fact that the noun is feminine because the subject is οὗτοί. The Byzantine text type appears to have read it as a predicate nominative, for it omits the article. The expression is difficult enough that without any textual support σπιλάδες ("reefs") is changed to σπίλοι ("blemishes") in some translations (NKJV, NAB, NIV, NRSV, but not NLT, NASB, ESV), perhaps because σπίλοι does indeed appear in the parallel in 2 Pet 2:13. The concept of "reef" implies both hiddenness and danger.

This negative predicate nominative or appositional element is followed by later appositional expressions: νεφέλαι ἄνυδροι, δένδρα φθινοπωρινά, κύματα ἄγρια θαλάσσῃ, and ἀστέρες πλανῆται.

οἱ ... συνευωχούμενοι. Pres mid ptc masc nom pl συνευωχέομαι (substantival). Predicate nominative. 𝔓[72] reads συνευχόμενοι ("praying together with"), likely because it was the more familiar term and sounded similar or because by the fourth century (it is a late third or early fourth-century papyrus) feasting together was no longer part of what a church did. The whole expression is amplified by Codex ℵ and C[2] with the addition before the participial phrase of γογγυσταὶ μεμψίμοιροι κατὰ τὰς (+ ἰδίας C[2]) ἐπιθυμίας αὐτῶν πορευόμενοι ("grumblers, complainers, going according to [their own] desires") from verse 16, with these uncials omitting the οἱ that begins the phrase.

ἀφόβως, ἑαυτοὺς ποιμαίνοντες. It is possible to take the adverb ἀφόβως with either this participial phrase or the preceding one. In the latter case, it would mean that they feast fearlessly or irreverently (without fear of God; cf. LXX Prov 15:16, where μετὰ φόβου κυρίου is contrasted with μετὰ ἀφοβίας). But Jude has a strong tendency to put adverbs before the participles that they modify rather than after them (vv. 3, 4, 8), so most likely this means "fearlessly shepherding/pasturing/feeding themselves."

ἑαυτούς. Accusative direct object of ποιμαίνοντες. 𝔓[72] reads αὐτούς with no change of meaning.

ποιμαίνοντες. Pres act ptc masc nom pl ποιμαίνω (substantival). This substantival participle is a nominative in apposition to οἱ ... συνευωχούμενοι, the predicate nominative.

νεφέλαι ἄνυδροι. Nominative in apposition to οἱ ... συνευωχούμενοι.

ὑπὸ ἀνέμων. Ultimate agency.

παραφερόμεναι. Pres pass ptc fem nom pl παραφέρω (attributive). The image (νεφέλαι ἄνυδροι ὑπὸ ἀνέμων παραφερόμεναι) may allude to Prov 25:14 (the LXX differs from the Hebrew, so this could be an allusion to the Hebrew text). 𝔓[72*] and B misunderstand that the previous structure has ended and so have the masculine nominative plural form παραφερόμενοι, which does not agree with νεφέλαι, rather than παραφερόμεναι (𝔓[72c] ℵ A C).

δένδρα φθινοπωρινὰ ἄκαρπα. Nominative in apposition to οἱ . . . συνευωχούμενοι. The adjective φθινοπωρινός ("belonging to late autumn") appears only here in the NT, whereas the adjective ἄκαρπος is more common, although usually it is used metaphorically in the NT. This and the previous image may well allude to imagery found in *1 Enoch* 80. The adjective ἄκαρπος occurs in *Jub.* 2.6; *4 Bar.* 9.16, and three other places in the Greek Pseudepigrapha, whereas φθινοπωρινός only occurs in line 18 of a fragment of Eusebius' *Historia Ecclesiastica* (7.32) found in Aristobulus, where it is used in a metaphorical sense.

δὶς. The adverb modifies ἀποθανόντα ("being dead"), perhaps referring to the outward "death" that comes in the late autumn and the death of being uprooted. It may, however, be an intensive expression that indicates "completely dead" or "doubly dead" similar to διπλῆς τιμῆς in 1 Tim 5:17.

ἀποθανόντα. Aor act ptc neut nom pl ἀποθνῄσκω (attributive).

ἐκριζωθέντα. Aor pass ptc neut nom pl ἐκριζόω. Nominative in apposition to ἀποθανόντα or perhaps adverbial, if the idea is that added to the deadness of fall they are also uprooted and thus "twice dead" ("being uprooted" or "since they are uprooted").

13 κύματα ἄγρια θαλάσσης ἐπαφρίζοντα τὰς ἑαυτῶν αἰσχύνας, ἀστέρες πλανῆται οἷς ὁ ζόφος τοῦ σκότους εἰς αἰῶνα τετήρηται.

The series of appositives from the previous verse continues: nominative noun + adjective + descriptive participle; then nominative noun + adjective + relative clause, rounding off the woe oracle and recalling the language of verse 6 in a rhetorical *inclusio*.

κύματα ἄγρια. Nominative in apposition to οἱ . . . συνευωχούμενοι. The adjective ἄγριος means "found in the open field" or "wild" (Friberg, 33), and only occurs elsewhere in the NT in Matt 3:4 and Mark 1:6. If this is an allusion to Isa 57:20, then Jude knows the Hebrew text (or an unknown Greek translation of it) since the LXX does not have the critical phrase.

θαλάσσης. Attributive genitive, if read as which type of wild waves, or possessive genitive, if read as the sea's waves, in this case wild ones.

ἐπαφρίζοντα. Pres act ptc neut nom pl ἐπαφρίζω (attributive).
τὰς ... αἰσχύνας. Accusative direct object of ἐπαφρίζοντα.
ἀστέρες πλανῆται. Nominative in apposition to οἱ ... σπιλάδες (or, alternatively, to οἱ ... συνευωχούμενοι). Rhetorically this is the last in a series denunciatory descriptions of the Others: "These are the A ... B ... B' ... A' ... A" ... A'" ... A"". Although this combination of the two nouns is common in Greek literature (BDAG, 822), πλανῆται appears only here in the NT and, here as elsewhere in the literature covered by BDAG, occurs in this expression. It refers to a wandering star or planet in contrast to the fixed stars, which remain in their proper places.
οἷς. Dative of disadvantage.
ὁ ζόφος. Nominative subject of τετήρηται. In verse 6, the angels are ὑπὸ ζόφον τετήρηκεν. Here, the Others are destined for "the gloom of darkness" or "dark gloom."
τοῦ σκότους. Attributive ("dark gloom") or epexegetical genitive ("the gloom, that is, the darkness"; so BDAG, 932.1; cf. BDF §167). The terms ζόφος and σκότους are close enough in meaning that 𝔓⁷² and B omit the first term.
εἰς αἰῶνα. This expression for "eternal" is far more common in the NT than ἀΐδιος (v. 6 and Rom 1:20 only).
τετήρηται. Prf pass ind 3rd sg τηρέω.

Jude 14-16

¹⁴And Enoch, the seventh (generation) from Adam, also prophesied about these, saying, "Look, the Lord comes with 10,000 of his holy ones ¹⁵to exercise judgment against all and to rebuke every being concerning all their impious deeds which they have impiously done and concerning all the hard things which impious sinners have spoken against him. ¹⁶These are grumblers, complainers, who live according to their own desires, and their mouths speak pompously, spouting insincere praise for the sake of (their own) benefit.

The prophecy Jude cites comes from *1 Enoch* 1:9, a prophecy about final judgment, which reads (Penner and Heiser):

⁹ Ὅτι ἔρχεται σὺν ταῖς μυριάσιν [αὐτοῦ καὶ τοῖς] ἁγίοις αὐτοῦ,
(a) ποιῆσαι κρίσιν κατὰ πάντων,
(b) καὶ ἀπολέσαι πάντας τοὺς ἀσεβεῖς,
(c) καὶ (ἐ)λέγξαι πᾶσαν σάρκα
(α) περὶ πάντων ἔργων τῆς ἀσεβείας αὐτῶν ὧν ἠσέβησαν
(β) καὶ σκληρῶν ὧν ἐλάλησαν λόγων κατ' αὐτοῦ ἁμαρτωλοὶ ἀσεβεῖς.

One quickly sees that while there are some differences, especially in the first line, the critical terms and grammatical relationships are in Jude with relatively minor differences. Jude is probably working from memory rather than a manuscript.

14 Προεφήτευσεν δὲ καὶ τούτοις ἕβδομος ἀπὸ Ἀδὰμ Ἑνὼχ λέγων, Ἰδοὺ ἦλθεν κύριος ἐν ἁγίαις μυριάσιν αὐτοῦ

Προεφήτευσεν... Ἑνώχ. Using a short introduction to indicate the prophet that he is citing, our author introduces a quotation from *1 Enoch* 1:9.

Προεφήτευσεν. Aor act ind 3rd sg προφητεύω. The position of the augment varies in the manuscripts: 𝔓⁷² and B* treat προ- as part of the verb stem rather than as a prepositional augment of the verb and thus read ἐπροφήτευσεν (see MHT, 2:192; BDF §69.4).

δὲ καὶ. The double particles δὲ καὶ (as in Matt 10:30; 1 John 1:3; see Friberg, 104) mark the transition to another voice, Enoch's.

τούτοις. Dative of reference with Προεφήτευσεν (cf. MHT, 3:238).

ἕβδομος. Nominative subject of Προεφήτευσεν. Ἕβδομος is an ordinal number (BDAG, 269). Thus, we are to understand "the seventh man" (descended) from Adam or perhaps "the seventh man from Adam" (in the genealogical lists).

Ἑνώχ. The indeclinable proper name is a nominative in apposition to ἕβδομος.

λέγων. Pres act ptc masc nom sg λέγω (manner). Here, the participial form of λέγω introduces a direct quotation just as ὅτι often introduces an indirect quotation (see v. 18). Thus, it is functionally equivalent to quotation marks in English.

Ἰδού. Strictly speaking the form should be ἰδού, "but [it appears] with an acute accent (ἰδού) when used as a demonstrative particle to prompt attention, followed by the nominative case to designate what is being pointed out" (Friberg, 202). In its use as an interjection, ἰδού is most common in Matthew, Luke/Acts, and Revelation. In derivation it is aor mid impv 2nd sg εἶδον.

ἦλθεν κύριος ἐν ἁγίαις μυριάσιν αὐτοῦ. The citation proper begins with ἦλθεν, a reference to the coming of the "king" and his "court," a rhetorically fitting way to mark the beginning of a judgment oracle. This singular use of an oracular form in Jude makes the quotation stand out. The use of the PP, ἐν ἁγίαις μυριάσιν αὐτοῦ, allows the whole court to be pictured while the singular verb and subject keep the focus on the one Lord.

ἦλθεν. Aor act ind 3rd sg ἔρχομαι. The use of the aorist is equivalent to the Hebrew prophetic perfect in which a future event is portrayed as complete.

κύριος. Nominative subject of ἦλθεν. Κύριος is ambiguous. The fact that it is anarthrous could suggest that it is being used as a proper name, but the article is also omitted in "formulae or set phrases . . . to which belong also titles, salutations, etc." (BDF §252.1). The term itself does not occur in *1 Enoch*, but the referent of the quotation is YHWH (see "The Great Holy One" in 1:3 and ὁ θεὸς τοῦ αἰῶνος in 1:4); in Jude (and other Christian contexts) the term could refer to His Sovereign Majesty Jesus (1:4), especially in a passage about his "coming" (e.g., Jas 5:7), even though in Jude 9 it probably refers to God the Father.

ἐν ἁγίαις μυριάσιν. Association.

αὐτοῦ. Genitive of possession.

15 ποιῆσαι κρίσιν κατὰ πάντων καὶ ἐλέγξαι πᾶσαν ψυχὴν περὶ πάντων τῶν ἔργων ἀσεβείας αὐτῶν ὧν ἠσέβησαν καὶ περὶ πάντων τῶν σκληρῶν ὧν ἐλάλησαν κατ' αὐτοῦ ἁμαρτωλοὶ ἀσεβεῖς.

The twofold purpose of the "coming" (in NT language, the Parousia) is expressed by two purpose infinitives, which are common with verbs of motion (BDF §390). The second infinitive expression is clearly the focus, for it is expanded with two περί phrases, each of which includes a relative clause. Stylistically, there is the repetition of versions of ἀσεβεία, first the noun itself, then the verb, and finally the adverb. The four-fold repetition of πᾶς is also striking. Both features come from *1 Enoch*.

ποιῆσαι κρίσιν. This expression is a Semitism. The Semitic idiom means that the active infinitive is used whereas in classical Greek the middle voice would have occurred (BDF §310.1).

ποιῆσαι. Aor act inf ποιέω (purpose).

κρίσιν. Accusative direct object of ποιῆσαι.

κατὰ πάντων. Opposition. The preposition κατά is used with the genitive, meaning "against," after verbs of hostile speech or action (BDAG, 511.I.2.b.β).

ἐλέγξαι. Aor act inf ἐλέγχω (purpose). Turner views this use of the verb as a Semitism (MHT, 4:139).

πᾶσαν ψυχὴν. Accusative object of ἐλέγξαι. Those convicted or reproved are every ψυχὴν, the term not being a contrast to some other part of the person, such as the body, but indicating the living being. The *1 Enoch* text has πᾶσαν σάρκα, which would emphasize mortality or creatureliness rather than living beings in contrast to inanimate creation. Some manuscripts (A B C) have πάντας τοὺς ἀσεβεῖς ("all the impious"), which was followed in 𝔐 by αὐτῶν, producing the text reflected in the KJV: "to convince all that are ungodly among them." This reading appears to be influenced by the multiple uses of the one root earlier. The NA²⁷/UBS⁴ text follows 𝔓⁷² and ℵ.

περὶ πάντων τῶν ἔργων. Reference. The predicate position of πάντων indicates that it means "all of the," rather than "the whole."

ἀσεβείας. Objective genitive. Jude piles up genitive nouns (lit. "concerning all of the works of impiety) rather than using an adjective here. Thus, ἀσεβείας is genitive singular rather than accusative plural.

αὐτῶν. Subjective genitive.

ὧν ἠσέβησαν. This pleonastic structure is also in *1 Enoch* 1:9.

ὧν. Genitive by attraction to τῶν ἔργων from the expected accusative (BDF §294.2).

ἠσέβησαν. Aor act ind 3rd pl ἀσεβέω.

περὶ πάντων τῶν σκληρῶν. Reference. Some manuscripts (ℵ C 33 *pc*) add λόγων at the end of this expression. The next clause will show that something spoken is understood, but no manuscripts of *1 Enoch* make the idea of λόγων explicit. The repetition of περὶ πάντων is a stylistic improvement that Jude has made to *1 Enoch*.

ὧν. Genitive by attraction to τῶν σκληρῶν.

ἐλάλησαν κατ' αὐτοῦ ἁμαρτωλοὶ ἀσεβεῖς. Speaking against [God] is certainly hostile, so we again have κατὰ with a verb of hostile speech or action (although one gets the hostility from context, not from the verb itself) as seen earlier in this verse. By putting the subject of the relative clause at the end, the rhetoric builds to a pleonastic climax.

ἐλάλησαν. Aor act ind 3rd pl λαλέω.

κατ' αὐτοῦ. Opposition (see above on κατὰ πάντων).

ἁμαρτωλοὶ ἀσεβεῖς. By putting the subject at the end of the sentence and the adjective after the noun, and highlighting the idea by using two words with an initial α sound, both *1 Enoch* and Jude gain rhetorical effect. The adjective ἀσεβής ("violating norms for a proper relation to deity, irreverent, impious, ungodly"; BDAG, 141) is normally used substantivally. Its meaning alone would constitute someone a "sinner." Thus the pleonastic expression ("impious sinner") highlights the level of impiety in view. With this flourish the quotation of *1 Enoch* 1:9 ends.

16 Οὗτοί εἰσιν γογγυσταὶ μεμψίμοιροι κατὰ τὰς ἐπιθυμίας ἑαυτῶν πορευόμενοι, καὶ τὸ στόμα αὐτῶν λαλεῖ ὑπέρογκα, θαυμάζοντες πρόσωπα ὠφελείας χάριν.

The emphatic Οὗτοι transitions from the quotation of *1 Enoch* back to the Others. Our author summarizes his concerns with a final set of charges. The same rhetorical strategy will be followed in verse 19 after an indirect quotation of those who evangelized these beloved believers.

Οὗτοί εἰσιν γογγυσταὶ μεμψίμοιροι. Using a predicate noun and a second noun in apposition to it, Jude accuses the Others of vices. Both nouns appear only here in the NT, and while the term γογγυστής does not occur in the LXX, three other forms of the root do, especially in the context of Israel in the wilderness, which has led some to posit an allusion to Israel (see MHT, 2:366). The word μεμψίμοιρος has a related term that appears in Col 3:13, but neither term nor their related verb appear in the LXX (see BDF §22). Thus there is no verbal connection to the LXX narratives of Israel in the wilderness.

Οὗτοί. Nominative subject of εἰσιν.

εἰσιν. Pres act ind 3rd pl εἰμί. Wallace (413) points to this as an example of the active voice used for stative action.

γογγυσταί. Predicate nominative.

Μεμψίμοιροι. Nominative in apposition to γογγυσταί.

κατὰ τὰς ἐπιθυμίας ἑαυτῶν πορευόμενοι. While A and C already had this phrase and the previous terms it modifies in verse 12, $\mathfrak{P}^{72}$ omits it altogether, perhaps thinking it an intrusion between two parts of a description concerning speech.

κατὰ τὰς ἐπιθυμίας. Standard.

πορευόμενοι. Pres mid ptc masc nom pl πορεύομαι (attributive). Jude continues his use of πορεύομαι for "living," "living in the manner of," "being directed by" (see v. 11, with this exact phrase being repeated in v. 18). This is, of course, a Semitic idiom. Given the anarthrous nature of the previous two nouns, the participial phrase should be read as adjectival, perhaps also an allusion to Israel in the wilderness.

καὶ τὸ στόμα αὐτῶν λαλεῖ ὑπέρογκα. They may complain (about God, the leadership of the community, or other things), but "their mouths" speak (a part-whole figure of speech, which is quite common in Hebrew literature).

τὸ στόμα. Nominative subject of λαλεῖ. The distributive use of the singular στόμα is typical of Greek—each "of them" has one στόμα. English speakers would say, "Their mouths."

ὑπέρογκα. The neuter plural of the adjective ὑπέρογκος appears in the NT only here and in its parallel in 2 Peter. However, it appears in Greek literature, including the LXX, Philo, and Josephus, meaning "of excessive size, puffed up, swollen." Used in reference to speech it means "haughty, pompous, bombastic" (BDAG, 1034).

λαλεῖ. Pres act ind 3rd sg λαλέω.

θαυμάζοντες πρόσωπα. This expression (lit. "amazing faces") appears to mean something similar to λαμβάνω plus πρόσωπον ("to show favoritism," Luke 20:21; Gal 2:6) or βλέπω plus πρόσωπον (Matt 18:10; Mark 12:14), perhaps "to curry favor."

θαυμάζοντες. Pres act ptc masc nom pl θαυμάζω (attendant circumstance). This verb was once strictly intransitive (the majority by far of its 43 occurrences in the NT) but can take an object, perhaps under the influence of the LXX (see Lev 19:15; Deut 10:17; Job 22:8; BDF §148.2; MHT, 3:244).

ὠφελείας χάριν. The word χάριν is an improper preposition meaning "for the sake of, on behalf of, on account of" (BDAG, 1078-79; BDF §160, 216). Here, it indicates the goal of the behavior. It generally follows the genitive noun that it governs (here, ὠφελείας).

Jude 17-19

[17]But you, loved ones, remember the words that the official delegates of our Lord, Jesus the Anointed One, previously told you, [18]that is, they used to say to you [that] at the end of time there will be mockers living according to their own impious desires. [19]These are those who cause divisions, are natural, (and) lack the Spirit.

17 Ὑμεῖς δέ, ἀγαπητοί, μνήσθητε τῶν ῥημάτων τῶν προειρημένων ὑπὸ τῶν ἀποστόλων τοῦ κυρίου ἡμῶν Ἰησοῦ Χριστοῦ

Ὑμεῖς ... ἀγαπητοί. The implied readers (the "loved ones") are addressed with a vocative (ἀγαπητοί) marking a transition, along with δέ, as Jude turns from his critique of the Others to his instruction of the "loved ones." The nominative subject pronoun Ὑμεῖς makes the shift more forceful.

μνήσθητε. Aor pass impv 2nd pl μιμνῄσκω. The call to remember serves two purposes: the rhetorical purpose of ethos in that it assumes that they already know this (cf. v. 5), and the appeal to tradition (versus the new revelation of the Others). Unlike the quotation from *1 Enoch* the words of these people are not written, so they must be remembered.

τῶν ῥημάτων. Genitive direct object of μνήσθητε. Verbs of remembering take a genitive object.

προειρημένων. Prf pass ptc masc gen pl προεῖπον (attributive). The lexical form προεῖπον is the second aorist since no present was in use at this period (Friberg, 328; BDAG, 867). The perfect fits well with the sense of something having been done with a continuing effect—words are not "unsaid" later. The point in stressing that these words were said previously is to point out that the Others were not a surprise either to God or to the leaders of his community and should not have been a surprise to the loved ones being addressed.

ὑπὸ τῶν ἀποστόλων. Ultimate agency. Having cited a scriptural prophecy, Jude now cites a more recent prophecy, one by "the official delegates of our Lord, Jesus the Anointed One," which could refer to the Twelve, other such official delegates of the period (e.g., Paul or James), or the church planters who planted that particular church. Note that ἀπόστολος is not a particularly religious word and was used by early Christians to mean "missionary" (*Didache* 11.3-6) or another type of "delegate" (2 Cor 8:23).

τοῦ κυρίου. Subjective genitive.

ἡμῶν. Genitive of subordination.

Ἰησοῦ Χριστοῦ. Genitive in apposition to τοῦ κυρίου. See also verse 1 on Χριστοῦ.

18 ὅτι ἔλεγον ὑμῖν· [ὅτι] ἐπ' ἐσχάτου [τοῦ] χρόνου ἔσονται ἐμπαῖκται κατὰ τὰς ἑαυτῶν ἐπιθυμίας πορευόμενοι τῶν ἀσεβειῶν.

The content of what is to be remembered is introduced by the second ὅτι and concerns the end of time when scoffers will be present (future) whose way of life is characterized by their living according to their own desires, which are in fact impious. This whole construction is grammatically difficult, perhaps because it does indeed go back to people who originally spoke in Aramaic.

ὅτι. The quotation of the official delegates appears to be "doubly introduced" by two uses of ὅτι. This first ὅτι, however, introduces a clause that is epexegetical to τῶν ῥημάτων.

ἔλεγον. Impf act ind 3rd pl λέγω. The purpose of the epexegetical ὅτι clause becomes clear here: Jude wants to clarify that the readers had already been told (προειρημένων) what he is about to say *on more than one occasion* (imperfect tense).

[ὅτι]. The second ὅτι introduces indirect discourse. The use of two instances of ὅτι so close together ($\mathfrak{P}^{72}$ A C P 33 𝔐 *al*) likely led to the omission of this one in some manuscripts (א B *pc*). One would expect some type of introduction of the indirect discourse, and there is no substitute for the missing ὅτι in the manuscripts that omit it. Thus the omission would be too difficult grammatically to be original and can be explained as the eye skipping over the second ὅτι due to the close proximity of the first one.

ἐπ' ἐσχάτου [τοῦ] χρόνου. Temporal (see BDF §234.8). The anarthrous ἐσχάτου is substantival (BDF §264.5), the whole expression ἐπ' ἐσχάτου [τοῦ] χρόνου being one of various ways the LXX has for rendering the Hebrew phrase meaning "in the afterward of days." Various attempts were made in the manuscript tradition to regularize this expression (the NA²⁷/UBS⁴ text is found in א A 33 *pc*) including: ἐν ἐσχάτῳ χρόνῳ ($\mathfrak{P}^{72vid}$ 𝔐) and ἐπ' ἐσχάτου χρόνου ($\mathfrak{P}^{72}$ B C *pc*).

ἔσονται. Fut mid ind 3rd pl εἰμί. The future tense fits well in the quotation, for it was indeed future from the point of view of those quoted, although present from Jude's point of view. Some manuscripts (א²A C² 33 *al*) change ἔσονται to ἐλεύσονται ("there will come").

ἐμπαῖκται. Nominative subject of ἔσονται. Given that this is a nominal agent formed from the verb ἐμπαίζω, one might expect the noun to follow the classical pattern of formation and end with –τήρ or –τωρ, but ἐμπαίκτης does not appear before Aristotle and so illustrates the later way such nouns were formed (MHT, 2:366).

κατὰ τὰς ἑαυτῶν ἐπιθυμίας. Standard. It is the behavior of these individuals, not the content of their mocking that is the focus here, unlike in 2 Pet 3:3 where the false teachers scoff about the Parousia and final judgment.

πορευόμενοι. Pres mid ptc masc nom pl πορεύομαι (attributive).

τῶν ἀσεβειῶν. Objective genitive. The noun ἀσέβεια means "godlessness," "irreverence," or "impiety" (BDAG, 141; Friberg, 77). The use of the plural form makes it clear that this noun is the object of their desires: "impious things," either because that is the character of what they desire or because the act of following one's desires makes the object of the desire godless (as happens in Jas 4:1-5). By putting τῶν ἀσεβειῶν last, Jude again stresses the highly immoral character of these individuals.

19 Οὗτοί εἰσιν οἱ ἀποδιορίζοντες, ψυχικοί, πνεῦμα μὴ ἔχοντες.

Οὗτοί. Nominative subject of εἰσιν. The emphatic and resumptive demonstrative (picking up on its previous uses in vv. 8, 10, 12, and 16) introduces three final predicate descriptions of the Others.

εἰσιν. Pres act ind 3rd pl εἰμί.

οἱ ἀποδιορίζοντες. Pres act ptc masc nom pl ἀποδιορίζω (substantival). Used only here in the NT, ἀποδιορίζω means to "separate" or "divide" (BDAG, 110). Thus, Jude may be saying, "these are the ones who cause a division." This is also the conclusion of Schmidt (455), though he reads the division against a putative Gnostic context of conflict between pneumatics and psychics. It is at least clear that the result of their teaching is division in the community, the opposite of ἐποικοδομοῦντες ἑαυτοὺς in verse 20. Yet it is possible that the scribe of Codex C (followed by the Vulgate and Augustine) may have correctly clarified the meaning by adding ἑαυτοὺς, i.e. they "separate themselves." This would give a rather neat parallelism and indicate that they formed themselves into a separate subgroup within the larger community pledged to Jesus.

ψυχικοί. Nominative in apposition to οἱ ἀποδιορίζοντες. The substantival adjective indicates that the Others are "natural" (Jas 3:15) or "physical" (1 Cor 15:44, 46), and thus unspiritual (see Schweizer, 663).

ἔχοντες. Pres act ptc masc nom pl ἔχω (substantival). Nominative in apposition to ψυχικοί. In his last descriptor, Jude uses a participial phrase to flesh out what ψυχικοί implies: the Others lack the eschatological gift of the Spirit. He does not indicate whether or not they once had it and lost it or whether they never had it; his point that climaxes this section is that they do not have it now (present tense, the participle giving the continuous aspect and the verb εἰσιν giving the time reference). The noun πνεῦμα is placed first in the phrase as an emphatic underlining of the implication of being ψυχικοί.

Jude 20-23

[20]But you, loved ones, by building yourselves up in your most holy faith, (and) praying in the Holy Spirit, [21]keep yourselves in

God's love as you await our Lord, Jesus the Anointed One's mercy resulting in eternal life. ²²And have mercy on those making distinctions, ²³and save some, snatching them from the fire; but have mercy on some in fear, hating even the chiton that is stained by the flesh.

Again, Jude transitions and addresses his "loved ones," this time not to tell them that the Others were to be expected (v. 17), but to tell them how to respond. The response is built around two imperatives, one a simple imperative (τηρήσατε) supported by circumstantial participles (collectively relating to the Spirit, Father, and "our Lord Jesus the Anointed One," and thus bearing witness to what would become the concept of the Trinity), and the second a series of three imperatives (ἐλεᾶτε ... σῴζετε ... ἐλεᾶτε), each one supported by an adverbial participle.

20 ὑμεῖς δέ, ἀγαπητοί, ἐποικοδομοῦντες ἑαυτοὺς τῇ ἁγιωτάτῃ ὑμῶν πίστει, ἐν πνεύματι ἁγίῳ προσευχόμενοι,

In Jude 19 the pronoun Οὗτοί referred to the Others in a final rhetorical summary. Here the contrasting pronoun (ὑμεῖς) plus δέ (functioning as an adversative in that the argument is moving forward a new topic of discussion, the reader's behavior) plus the vocative ἀγαπητοί ("beloved," "loved ones") is used to mark a new focus and a new paragraph. The main verb and thus the main point of the paragraph comes in the next verse, τηρήσατε. In verse 20 we have two circumstantial participles (although some might argue that this is an imperatival use of the participle) that describe how the group is to do this: unified strengthening of their commitment and prayer in the Spirit (the same Spirit that the Others lack).

ὑμεῖς δέ, ἀγαπητοί. Jude repeats the exact same form of address as in verse 17.

ὑμεῖς. Nominative subject of τηρήσατε (v. 21). See also verse 17.

ἀγαπητοί. Vocative. See also verse 17.

ἐποικοδομοῦντες. Pres act ptc masc nom pl ἐποικοδομέω (means or attendant circumstance). The verb means to "build on" or "build further" upon a foundation or previous structure

(BDAG, 387). While it is often used in a metaphorical sense in the NT, it is usually passive (Eph 2:20; Col 2:7; 1 Pet 2:5). Here it is active and modified by the reflexive pronoun ἑαυτοὺς ("building up yourselves"). They are to build themselves, strengthen themselves, or even unite themselves (if one thinks of building a stronger and more unified structure as the metaphor). On the verb form, see also Michel, 147-48.

ἑαυτοὺς. Accusative direct object of ἐποικοδομοῦντες.

τῇ ἁγιωτάτῃ ... πίστει. Dative of reference. The phrase could be rendered "most holy commitment," assuming that πίστει implies commitment to Jesus or commitment to follow Jesus, rather than a set of beliefs about Jesus (see Bultmann, 173-277). The use of the superlative is quite normal in classical Greek (Wallace, 202-3), although the superlative is dying out in Koine Greek by the time of the NT. Here, ἁγιωτάτῃ, one of four true superlatives in the NT, carries elative force (BDF §60). The designation "most holy" or "emphatically holy" contrasts with the impiety that is repeatedly attributed to the Others, who have by their actions denied their commitment to Jesus as Lord.

ὑμῶν. Subjective genitive.

ἐν πνεύματι ἁγίῳ προσευχόμενοι. This could be read as a second means of keeping themselves in God's love or as an attendant circumstance or means of building themselves up in the faith. The former reading seems more likely.

προσευχόμενοι. Pres mid ptc masc nom pl προσεύχομαι (means or attendant circumstance). 𝔓[72] adds ἑαυτοῖς ("for yourselves") in what looks like a case of dittography given the following ἑαυτοὺς.

ἐν πνεύματι. Sphere ("in the sphere of the Holy Spirit") or instrumental ("by means of the Holy Spirit" or "using (the power) of the Holy Spirit"). There are parallels in Paul, such as 1 Cor 12:3, which refers to some type of ecstatic word as speaking "in the Spirit," and 1 Thess 1:5, which contrasts ἐν λόγῳ μόνον with ἐν δυνάμει καὶ ἐν πνεύματι ἁγίῳ. The latter seems to point to speech in the power of or marked by the action of the Spirit. The loved ones can and should pray under the influence of the Spirit in contrast to the Others who do not have the Spirit.

21 ἑαυτοὺς ἐν ἀγάπῃ θεοῦ τηρήσατε προσδεχόμενοι τὸ ἔλεος τοῦ κυρίου ἡμῶν Ἰησοῦ Χριστοῦ εἰς ζωὴν αἰώνιον.

ἑαυτούς. Accusative direct object of τηρήσατε. Fronted for emphasis.

ἐν ἀγάπῃ. Dative of sphere. Thus, the whole expression means "do not stray outside the love of God." Note that ἀγάπη does not refer to feelings, but rather to caring actions, as in most NT contexts.

θεοῦ. The genitive could be either objective ("your love for God") or subjective ("God's love for you"). The focus here on "keeping" and the preceding context that speaks of Others who have strayed into an area where they are clearly not loved by God (v. 13) makes the subjective genitive more likely (so BDAG, 1002.2.b; contra Wallace, 121, n. 136, who calls it a plenary genitive), with the reference then having eschatological overtones. MHT (4:140) views the lack of an article here as a Semitism influenced by the Hebrew construct state.

τηρήσατε. Aor act impv 2nd pl τηρέω. The verb τηρέω is used five times in Jude (70 times in the NT as a whole, including four times in the longer 2 Peter), usually with God as the stated or implied agent. This is the one time that they are called to keep or guard something and that something is themselves. Some important manuscripts ($\mathfrak{P}^{72}$ B C*vid Ψ pc) read τηρήσωμεν ("let us keep ourselves"), which is inconsistent with the second person reference (ὑμεῖς) in both verses 17 and 20 and the second person imperatives that follow in verses 22 and 23.

προσδεχόμενοι. Pres mid ptc masc nom pl προσδέχομαι (temporal). The final participial phrase of the sentence, a circumstantial participle, gives the attitude they are to have as they keep themselves in God's love. Since the object of the participle is not personal, the attitude described is that of "awaiting," "expecting," or "looking for."

τὸ ἔλεος. Accusative direct object of προσδεχόμενοι.

τοῦ κυρίου. Subjective genitive.

ἡμῶν. Genitive of subordination.

Ἰησοῦ. Genitive in apposition to τοῦ κυρίου.

Χριστοῦ. Genitive in apposition to Ἰησοῦ (see v. 1).

εἰς ζωὴν αἰώνιον. Goal or result (cf. BDAG, 290.4.e). The Lord's mercy in the final judgment results in/leads to that quality of life that is described as eternal life. This contrasts with the lack of mercy for the fallen angels and the Others and the prediction of destruction for them. 𝔓⁷² reads εἰς ζωὴν ἡμῶν Ἰησοῦ Χριστοῦ αἰώνιον.

22 καὶ οὓς μὲν ἐλεᾶτε διακρινομένους,

καὶ. The conjunction links this imperative to the previous one (τηρήσατε, v. 21).

οὓς μὲν. Accusative direct object of ἐλεᾶτε. Relative pronouns are sometimes used with μέν and δέ to construct lists, a non-classical use known elsewhere in the NT (MHT, 3:36; BDF §250): "some ... others." Robertson (695–96) calls this a demonstrative use of the relative pronoun with μέν and δέ. Here, as in Matt 13:8, 23; 21:35; and 25:15, the list has three components: ὅς μὲν ... ὅς δὲ ... ὅς δὲ ("some ... others ... others"). The problem with the series is that the verb (ἐλεᾶτε) in the οὓς μὲν clause is repeated in the second ὅς δὲ clause but not in the first one which makes it unlike any of the lists cited above, which either have the same verb understood in all three elements or use different verbs in each of the elements. It is possible that the text has an aposiopesis, the omission of the main clause that should go with the second οὓς δὲ, either because it is understood from context or because it dropped out in transmission (BDF §482). It is perhaps more likely that all three clauses refer to the same group with the ὅς μὲν ... ὅς δὲ ... ὅς δὲ construction moving the thought along to what is, perhaps, Jude's main point: be careful during your rescue operation. Some manuscripts appear to read the repeated words as a dittography or else unconsciously create a haplography, either dropping the first οὓς δὲ (B) or the second (𝔐). The NA²⁷/UBS⁴ text follows ℵ A Ψ 33 *al.*

ἐλεᾶτε. Pres act impv 2nd pl ἐλεάω. This verb has the "same meaning as ἐλεέω, serving as the present-tense by-form" (Friberg, 142), and is changed to ἐλεέω in 𝔐, while 𝔓⁷² omits the term. For more on the form, see MHT, 2:195–96. The beloved ones expect to receive mercy (τὸ ἔλεος, v. 21), so it is not surprising that they are called on (imperative) here to exercise mercy (ἐλεᾶτε). The concept of having mercy appears to have been difficult for some communities (A C 33 *pm* have ἐλέγχετε, "rebuke" or "convict").

διακρινομένους. Pres mid ptc masc acc pl διακρίνω (attributive). The unusual example of a participle modifying a relative expression (οὓς μὲν) likely led to the textual variants: 𝔐 and many other manuscripts use the nominative διακρινόμενοι, which would then be adverbial ("as you make a distinction" or "as you contend"). The meaning of the verb, however, is also difficult to determine. The clause means either "have mercy on those making distinctions" (following the usual figurative meaning of διακρίνω in the NT: "to make a distinction between persons") or, "have mercy on those who are contending" or possibly "doubting" (a normal sense in the middle, see v. 9; so Büchsel 946). The sense "doubting," however, is not convincing since (a) this meaning is apparently first found in the NT, making it a novel usage, and (b) Jude has already used the term with the normal meaning of "contend." In other words, what Jude appears to be saying is that one should have mercy on the Others, those who are making divisions (equivalent to making distinctions) in verse 19, those who are contending about what commitment to Jesus looks like (perhaps equivalent to the scoffing/mocking of v. 18). The fact that this was not the response to the Others that scribes in the third and fourth centuries expected may also have led to the nominative variant.

23 οὓς δὲ σῴζετε ἐκ πυρὸς ἁρπάζοντες, οὓς δὲ ἐλεᾶτε ἐν φόβῳ μισοῦντες καὶ τὸν ἀπὸ τῆς σαρκὸς ἐσπιλωμένον χιτῶνα.

οὓς δὲ. Accusative direct object of σῴζετε. The οὓς δὲ gives the next step in having mercy.

σῴζετε. Pres act impv 2nd pl σῴζω. The command is to deliver or save "those who contend" (with the participle from v. 22 implied). On the one hand, the readers are to have mercy. On the other hand, they are not to leave them the way they are, but to save them, snatching them out of the fire (so that they will no longer be οὓς . . . διακρινομένους).

ἐκ πυρὸς. Separation. The PP likely modifies ἁρπάζοντες since σῴζετε has its needed object in οὓς δὲ and ἁρπάζοντες requires some reference as to where to snatch them from.

ἁρπάζοντες. Pres act ptc masc nom pl ἁρπάζω (means).

οὓς δὲ ἐλεᾶτε. Accusative direct object of ἐλεᾶτε. The repetition of ἐλεᾶτε with οὓς δὲ is surprising if we have three different groups of people. This likely resumes the previous imperatives and advances the thought to the manner of fulfillment.

ἐλεᾶτε. Pres act impv 2nd pl ἐλεάω. On the form, see verse 22.

ἐν φόβῳ. Manner.

μισοῦντες. Pres act ptc masc nom pl μισέω (means). How one expresses mercy ἐν φόβῳ is described by the participial phrase.

καὶ. Adverbial, ascensive: "even."

τὸν . . . χιτῶνα. Accusative direct object of μισοῦντες. The χιτών, or chiton, is an article of Greek clothing worn by both men and women next to the body. The ἱμάτιον, on the other hand, was worn outside the chiton for warmth. The singular is used here in the distributive sense, for each of the Others wore a (literal as well as a) metaphorical chiton.

ἀπὸ τῆς σαρκὸς. Agency.

ἐσπιλωμένον. Prf pass ptc masc acc sg σπιλόω (attributive). The chiton has been stained (perfect) by the flesh (body), which would be true of literal chitons, and in this case is true of the metaphorical chiton of those who have been driven by desire.

Jude 24-25

²⁴To the One who is able to keep you faultless and make you stand blameless in joy in the presence of his honor, ²⁵to the only God our Deliverer through Jesus the Anointed One our Lord be honor, majesty, sovereignty, and dominion before all the ages and now and unto all the ages. Amen.

Rhetorically, the *peroratio* of the letter, i.e., the summary and conclusion of the letter argument, finished with verse 23. What one would expect now would be a letter ending, which in the case of Jude includes only one element: a health wish-prayer cast in the form of a doxology.

24 Τῷ δὲ δυναμένῳ φυλάξαι ὑμᾶς ἀπταίστους καὶ στῆσαι κατενώπιον τῆς δόξης αὐτοῦ ἀμώμους ἐν ἀγαλλιάσει,

Τῷ δὲ δυναμένῳ φυλάξαι ὑμᾶς ἀπταίστους. Text critically it should be noted that K P 𝔐 miss the form of the doxology and make it impersonal by changing ὑμᾶς to αὐτούς, whereas A makes it inclusive by changing it to ἡμᾶς, which fits the context, especially Jude 25, although the text as printed fits the previous verse and is better supported by the manuscript evidence.

Τῷ ... δυναμένῳ. Pres mid ptc masc dat sg δύναμαι (substantival). Dative of possession. As usual, the stereotyped liturgical formula for a doxology uses a dative NP without a main verb (see also BDF §128.5; MHT, 3:296–97). Some form of the verb εἰμί is understood, probably a voluntative optative (see Wallace, 481–83).

δὲ. The δέ, Jude's favorite linking term, introduces the letter's closing prayer (a typical part of a Greek letter ending).

φυλάξαι. Aor act inf φυλάσσω (complementary). φυλάσσω ("keeping" or "guarding") involves a positive sense here (although φυλάσσω has an overlapping semantic field with τηρέω) and is followed by an object-complement double accusative (Wallace, 182).

ὑμᾶς. Accusative direct object of φυλάξαι.

ἀπταίστους. Complement in an object-complement double accusative construction. This verbal adjective (on the form, see BDF §117.1) occurs only here in the NT (MHT, 4:139; see also 3 Macc 6:39) and in this context describes the quality of the guarding, the sense in which one is kept or protected, namely not stumbling in the moral sense (BDAG, 126), free from falling from commitment to Jesus (see Stählin, 756: "[May God] keep you [to the end] as those who do not fall").

στῆσαι. Aor act inf ἵστημι (complementary). The direct object ὑμᾶς is understood.

κατενώπιον τῆς δόξης. Adverbial PP, which consists of the improper preposition κατενώπιον (BDF §214.5), which is probably a Septuagintalism (MHT, 4:140; cf. MHT, 3:277), and the expression τῆς δόξης αὐτοῦ, which is a circumlocution for God himself, a function that is common for δόξα.

αὐτοῦ. Subjective genitive.

ἀμώμους. Complement in an object-complement double accusative construction. The adjective refers to "perfect moral and religious piety" (Hauck, 831). The form is built like ἀπταίστους with an alpha privative and thus forms a lovely parallel in this second member of the construction with a pleasing rhetorical symmetry. Codex A reads ἀμέμπτους ("blameless").

ἐν ἀγαλλιάσει. Manner: "with gladness, (extreme) joy, feeling of great happiness" (Friberg, 30). The PP probably modifies στῆσαι (how one stands), but if it modifies ἀμώμους (the stance in which one is blameless) it would be locative.

25 μόνῳ θεῷ σωτῆρι ἡμῶν διὰ Ἰησοῦ Χριστοῦ τοῦ κυρίου ἡμῶν δόξα μεγαλωσύνη κράτος καὶ ἐξουσία πρὸ παντὸς τοῦ αἰῶνος καὶ νῦν καὶ εἰς πάντας τοὺς αἰῶνας, ἀμήν.

The final verse of the letter clarifies who is intended by "the one who is able" in verse 24 with the appositional μόνῳ θεῷ σωτῆρι ἡμῶν. It then goes on to describe that which is wished for or ascribed to this divinity and ends with the liturgical "amen."

μόνῳ θεῷ. Dative in apposition to Τῷ ... δυναμένῳ (v. 24). The combination of the adjective μόνῳ with θεῷ makes it clear that the Jewish God is intended, the only God (no article is needed with God, for God functions as a proper noun). 𝔐 adds the adjective σοφῷ.

σωτῆρι. Dative in apposition to μόνῳ θεῷ. The term σωτήρ was a common title for the emperor and other rescuers, including divine ones. In the NT, it is usually attributed to Jesus (Jesus as Lord/Savior versus the emperor as Lord/Savior), but in Jude only to God the Father.

ἡμῶν. Objective genitive.

διὰ Ἰησοῦ Χριστοῦ. Intermediate agent. See also verse 1 on Χριστοῦ.

τοῦ κυρίου. Genitive in apposition to Ἰησοῦ Χριστοῦ.

ἡμῶν. Genitive of subordination.

δόξα μεγαλωσύνη κράτος καὶ ἐξουσία. Nominative subject of an implied verb. While there is some variation in the manuscripts, especially 𝔓⁷² and 𝔐, what is attributed to God through Jesus is generally understood as a series of honor words. The term δόξα essentially means "honor" (thus the addition of τιμή to the list by 𝔓⁷² is probably a pleonastic amplification), and it is underlined by μεγαλωσύνη ("majesty" or "greatness"; used only of God, as here and in Heb 1:3; 8:1), κράτος ("power" or "imperial dominion," implying dominion through force or strength; Friberg, 236) and ἐξουσία ("authority," i.e., the right to rule).

πρὸ παντὸς τοῦ αἰῶνος καὶ νῦν καὶ εἰς πάντας τοὺς αἰῶνας. The duration of the attribution is indicated through the three phases of time ranging from protology through the present to the eschaton.

πρὸ παντὸς τοῦ αἰῶνος. Temporal (see Wallace, 379). The predicate position of παντὸς results in "before all the ages," rather than "before the whole of the ages."

νῦν. The καὶ . . . καὶ construction keeps the νῦν from being understood as anything other than another member of the three stages of time (cf. Delling, "τρεῖς, τρίς, τρίτος," 225).

εἰς πάντας τοὺς αἰῶνας. Temporal ("unto" or "throughout"). On πάντας, see above on πρὸ παντὸς τοῦ αἰῶνος. Here, the plural αἰῶνας reflects a Semitism first found in the LXX (MHT, 3:25).

ἀμήν. A transliterated form of a Hebrew term used liturgically. When translated rather than transliterated in the LXX, γένοιτο is typically used ("let it be so," "truly"; Friberg, 46).

2 Peter

2 Peter 1:1-2

¹Simon Peter, slave and apostle of Jesus the Anointed One, to those who have received an allegiance equally precious to ours by the righteous action of our God and Savior, Jesus the Anointed One. ²May grace and peace be abundantly yours in the knowledge of God and Jesus our Lord.

1:1 Συμεὼν Πέτρος δοῦλος καὶ ἀπόστολος Ἰησοῦ Χριστοῦ τοῖς ἰσότιμον ἡμῖν λαχοῦσιν πίστιν ἐν δικαιοσύνῃ τοῦ θεοῦ ἡμῶν καὶ σωτῆρος Ἰησοῦ Χριστοῦ,

The form of the salutation is precisely what is expected: writer in the nominative, recipients in the dative. In this case the recipient is indicated by a substantival participle, which allows for the addition of an object and adverbial modifiers.

Συμεὼν Πέτρος δοῦλος καὶ ἀπόστολος. The string of nominative singular nouns, first proper names, then appositive titles joined by καί, is a more typical structure than what is found in Jude 1.

Συμεὼν Πέτρος. Nominative absolute. Some manuscripts ($\mathfrak{P}^{72}$ B Ψ *pm*) have the more usual Hellenized spelling Σίμων (BDF §53.2) rather than the transliterated Συμεών. Outside of the reference to the tribe of Simeon in Rev 7:7, this form appears only here and in Acts 15:14, where it also refers to Peter. It is not surprising that some scribes shifted to the more normal spelling.

δοῦλος καὶ ἀπόστολος. Nominative in apposition to Συμεὼν Πέτρος.

Ἰησοῦ Χριστοῦ. Objective genitive in relation to δοῦλος (Peter serves Jesus) and subjective genitive in relation to ἀπόστολος (Jesus sends Peter). See also Jude 1 on Χριστοῦ.

τοῖς ... λαχοῦσιν. Aor act ptc masc dat pl λαγχάνω (substantival). Dative of recipient.

ἰσότιμον ... πίστιν. Accusative direct object of λαχοῦσιν. In a Christian context like this πίστις means "acceptance of the kerygma about Christ" (Bultmann, 208); the term can often be translated "firm commitment" (BDAG, 819.2.b.δ), "trust" (BDAG,

818.2), "faithful or loyal" (BDAG 818.1.a), or even as an "oath" or "troth" (BDAG, 818.1.b). The problem with "faith" as a gloss is that it has too many mental religious overtones in English and tends to be associated with doctrines believed versus a person or kingdom committed to. The kerygma in general, and especially the version assumed by 2 Peter and Jude, presents Jesus as Lord. The translation "allegiance," which brings to mind the parallel notion of allegiance to an earthly ruler, is thus especially fitting, since it contains the appropriate sense of trust and commitment implied in the Greek term.

ἰσότιμον. A NT *hapax legomenon*, meaning "equal in honor/value" (BDAG, 481), fronted to stress their equal privilege with the author.

ἡμῖν. Dative complement of ἰσότιμον (see also BDF §194.1).

ἐν δικαιοσύνῃ. Instrumental. Codex ℵ has εἰς δικαιοσύνην, indicating that the commitment or faith had the goal of divine righteousness.

τοῦ θεοῦ ἡμῶν καὶ σωτῆρος Ἰησοῦ Χριστοῦ. This phrase is a *crux interpretum*. The syntax of τοῦ θεοῦ . . . καὶ σωτῆρος is an example of the Granville Sharp Rule: two nouns (θεοῦ and σωτῆρος) that are personal but not proper names, are in the same case, and are preceded by a definite article that is not repeated before the second noun refer to the same person (see also v. 11). Here, that person is then identified as Ἰησοῦ Χριστοῦ, who is thus described as both "God" and "Savior" (see the discussion in Wallace, 270–77; MHT, 3:181; 1:84). While these titles would not have been that unusual used for kings, Codex ℵ and several later manuscripts and versions conformed this phrase to more usual statements about Jesus by using κυρίου instead of θεοῦ.

τοῦ θεοῦ . . . καὶ σωτῆρος. Subjective genitive. Our God and Savior has performed righteous acts.

ἡμῶν. Genitive of subordination.

Ἰησοῦ Χριστοῦ. Genitive in apposition to τοῦ θεοῦ . . . καὶ σωτῆρος. See also Jude 1 on Χριστοῦ.

1:2 χάρις ὑμῖν καὶ εἰρήνη πληθυνθείη ἐν ἐπιγνώσει τοῦ θεοῦ καὶ Ἰησοῦ τοῦ κυρίου ἡμῶν.

The typical Greek greeting was χαίρειν, as in Jas 1:1; and Paul normally changes this to χάρις. Second Peter is more like Paul in that instead of Jude's more elaborate triple greeting he uses only χάρις καὶ εἰρήνη, the latter probably developing from the Jewish greeting *shalom*.

χάρις ... καὶ εἰρήνη. Nominative subject of πληθυνθείη.

ὑμῖν. Dative indirect object of πληθυνθείη or dative of advantage.

πληθυνθείη. Aor pass opt 3rd sg πληθύνω. The nominative noun indicating the blessing plus the dative indicating the recipient of the blessing was sufficient, with the verb being assumed, as in Paul's usage in 1 Cor 1:3: χάρις ὑμῖν καὶ εἰρήνη. Here there is an explicit verb. The optative is used for a wish or prayer. Using an explicit verb, as here, increases the emphatic nature of the blessing over the more typical use of an implied verb ("may X be ..."). The passive structure, which implies God will do the multiplying, may indicate a Jewish tendency not to name God in such formulas, although this probably became unreflective normal usage in the Jesus movement.

ἐν ἐπιγνώσει. Sphere ("in"), cause ("because of"), or instrument ("by"). The noun ἐπίγνωσις means "knowledge, acknowledgment, recognition" (Friberg, 163; cf. BDAG, 369), and thus implies more than just "knowing about" something.

τοῦ θεοῦ καὶ Ἰησοῦ. Objective genitive. The Granville-Sharp Rule would not apply here despite the single article, since one of the nouns is a proper name. However, the similarity to 2 Pet 1:1 probably lies behind textual issues: Some later manuscripts have dropped the τοῦ, making it clear that θεοῦ and Ἰησοῦ are two separate beings; $\mathfrak{P}^{72}$ leaves out καὶ Ἰησοῦ, reducing the reference to a single being, possibly referring to Jesus as "God our Lord"; and ℵ and A give Jesus his full title (Ἰησοῦ Χριστοῦ), conforming the usage to 2 Pet 2:1.

τοῦ κυρίου. Genitive in apposition to Ἰησοῦ.

ἡμῶν. Genitive of subordination.

2 Peter 1:3-11

³In that his divine power has given to us everything leading to life and godliness by means of the knowledge of the one who

called us by his own glory and virtue, ⁴through which he has given us precious and fantastic promises so that through them we may become sharers in the divine nature, having fled from the corruption that is in the world in desire, ⁵and with respect to this, making every effort, in your commitment supply excellence of character, in your excellence of character knowledge, ⁶in your knowledge self-control, in your self-control patient endurance, in your patient endurance piety, ⁷in your piety affectionate commitment to your (Christian) siblings, and in your affectionate commitment to your (Christian) siblings love. ⁸For if these things are present and increasing in you, they will make (you) neither useless nor unfruitful with respect to the knowledge of our Lord Jesus the Anointed One; ⁹for the one in whom these things are not present is blind, is nearsighted, since they have forgotten the cleansing of their past sins. ¹⁰Therefore, rather, brothers and sisters, be eager to make your calling and election firm; for if you do these things you will certainly never stumble. ¹¹For thus entrance into the eternal kingdom of our Lord and Savior Jesus the Anointed One will be richly provided for you.

1:3 Ὡς πάντα ἡμῖν τῆς θείας δυνάμεως αὐτοῦ τὰ πρὸς ζωὴν καὶ εὐσέβειαν δεδωρημένης διὰ τῆς ἐπιγνώσεως τοῦ καλέσαντος ἡμᾶς ἰδίᾳ δόξῃ καὶ ἀρετῇ,

Structurally, this is a difficult verse. There is no indicative verb until verse 4, and it occurs in a relative clause. The main verb of the sentence does not come until verse 5, as will be seen. What is clear is that although verses 3-4 are theologically very interesting to modern interpreters, the author puts the grammatical focus on verse 5, in line with the theme of the letter.

Ὡς. Here, ὡς is used with a participle to give the reason for an action (see BDAG, 1105.3.a.β). It is debated whether the phrase this introduces is an anacoluthon, resumed with καὶ αὐτὸ τοῦτο δὲ in verse 5 (Zerwick, 717), or whether it is grammatically an expansion of verse 2 (*Lexham*; Bauckham, 173).

πάντα ... τὰ πρὸς ζωὴν καὶ εὐσέβειαν. Accusative direct object of δεδωρημένης.

πρὸς ζωὴν καὶ εὐσέβειαν. The basic meaning of the preposition with the accusative is a "marker of movement or orientation toward" a person or thing (BDAG, 875.3), hence "leading to," rather than the specific translations suggested by BDAG (875.3.e.β), i.e., "with regard to," "as far as (life and piety) is concerned," "what makes for."

τῆς θείας δυνάμεως. Genitive subject of δεδωρημένης. The adjective ("divine") is Hellenistic, and is found in the NT only here, verse 4, and in Acts 17:29.

αὐτοῦ. Subjective genitive.

δεδωρημένης. Prf mid ptc fem gen sg δωρέομαι. Genitive absolute, used with ὡς in a causal construction (see above).

διὰ τῆς ἐπιγνώσεως. Means.

τοῦ καλέσαντος. Aor act ptc masc gen sg καλέω (substantival). Objective genitive.

ἰδίᾳ δόξῃ καὶ ἀρετῇ. Dative of instrument or respect. The word pair is a "stock combination of Hellenistic writers" (Bauckham, 178). Some important manuscripts ($\mathfrak{P}^{72}$ B 𝔐 *pm*) read διὰ δόξης καὶ ἀρετῆς. This reading may have been influenced by the preceding διά + genitive phrase, or it could reflect an effort to make the instrumental sense more explicit. The NA^{27}/UBS^4 text is found in ℵ A C 33 *pm*.

1:4 δι' ὧν τὰ τίμια καὶ μέγιστα ἡμῖν ἐπαγγέλματα δεδώρηται, ἵνα διὰ τούτων γένησθε θείας κοινωνοὶ φύσεως ἀποφυγόντες τῆς ἐν τῷ κόσμῳ ἐν ἐπιθυμίᾳ φθορᾶς.

δι' ὧν. Means. The antecedent is ἰδίᾳ δόξῃ καὶ ἀρετῇ.

τὰ τίμια καὶ μέγιστα ... ἐπαγγέλματα. Accusative direct object of δεδώρηται.

ἡμῖν. Dative indirect object of δεδώρηται or dative of reference. The awkward placement of ἡμῖν led to several variants: τίμια καὶ μέγιστα ἐπαγγέλματα ἡμῖν ($\mathfrak{P}^{72}$), τίμια ἡμῖν καὶ μέγιστα ἐπαγγέλματα (ℵ 𝔐 *pc*), and μέγιστα καὶ τίμια ἡμῖν ἐπαγγέλματα (A C 33 *pm*). The NA^{27}/UBS^4 text is found in B and a few other manuscripts.

Μέγιστα. Here, the superlative form of μέγας is used where one would expect the elative, but that is a common use of the superative in the NT (BDF §60. 2; cf. Wallace, 303; on the form, see MHT, 2:165).

δεδώρηται. Prf mid ind 3rd sg δωρέομαι.

ἵνα. Purpose-result ἵνα clause (Wallace, 473–74).

διὰ τούτων. Means, the fourth example of this construction in verses 3-4. In this case the antecedent is ἐπαγγέλματα.

γένησθε. Aor mid subj 2nd pl γίνομαι. Subjunctive with ἵνα. Notice the shift from first plural pronoun (ἡμῖν) to second plural verb here.

θείας ... φύσεως. Objective genitive. The noun κοινωνός is sometimes used with a dative NP or a PP (see BDAG, 553–54; BDF §182). The adjective θείας ("divine") modifies the noun φύσεως ("nature") and it also appears to be fronted for emphasis.

ἀποφυγόντες. Aor act ptc masc nom pl ἀποφεύγω (temporal). The circumstantial participle indicates an event previous to the verb it modifies.

τῆς ἐν τῷ κόσμῳ ἐν ἐπιθυμίᾳ φθορᾶς. There is a textual issue relating to the last two words and the repeated ἐν. The NA²⁷/UBS⁴ text is found in A and B. The same text appears in 𝔐 without the τῷ (κόσμος is frequently anarthrous; see BDF §253.4). Many manuscripts (C Ψ *pm*) omit the second ἐν (an understandable instance of haplography). On the other hand, 𝔓⁷² reads ἀποφυγόντες τὴν ἐν τῷ κόσμῳ ἐπιθυμίαν φθοράν, while ℵ reads ἀποφυγόντες τὴν ἐν τῷ κόσμῳ ἐπιθυμίαν φθορᾶς. The shift in case likely simply reflects the fact that ἀποφυγόντες can take either a genitive or accusative modifier (BDAG, 125; note the use of the accusative in 2:18, 20).

τῆς ... φθορᾶς. Genitive complement of ἀποφυγόντες.

ἐν τῷ κόσμῳ. Locative.

ἐν ἐπιθυμίᾳ. Cause or instrumental.

1:5 καὶ αὐτὸ τοῦτο δὲ σπουδὴν πᾶσαν παρεισενέγκαντες ἐπιχορηγήσατε ἐν τῇ πίστει ὑμῶν τὴν ἀρετήν, ἐν δὲ τῇ ἀρετῇ τὴν γνῶσιν,

αὐτὸ τοῦτο. Accusative of respect. This phrase ("this very thing") appears 9 times in the New Testament, usually with εἰς (Rom 9:17; 13:6; 2 Cor 5:5; Eph 6:22; Col 4:8) or as a verbal object

(Gal 2:10; Phil 1:6), although it can also occur as a nominative neuter subject (2 Cor 7:11). Here it appears to be an accusative of respect resuming the participation in the divine nature of the previous verse: "just for this reason" or "with respect to this very thing" (MHT, 3:45). It is unusual enough that it was sometimes misread, with many manuscripts (ℵ C² Ψ 33 *pm*) moving δὲ to its usual position: αὐτὸ δὲ τοῦτο; a few manuscripts leaving out the δέ entirely; Codex A reading αὐτοὶ δὲ; and most manuscripts supporting the NA²⁷/UBS⁴ reading (𝔓⁷² B C* 𝔐 *pc*). BDF (§290.4) finds this expression difficult enough to suggest that it may have originally read κατ' αὐτὸ δὲ τοῦτο.

παρεισενέγκαντες. Aor act ptc masc nom pl παρεισφέρω (means).

σπουδὴν πᾶσαν. Accusative direct object of παρεισενέγκαντες. Idiomatic for "bring every effort to," or "do one's very best to" (Friberg, 299).

ἐπιχορηγήσατε. Aor act impv 2nd pl ἐπιχορηγέω.

ἐν τῇ πίστει ὑμῶν τὴν ἀρετήν. The repetitive structure that follows (7 iterations) is an example of "grand style" that is viewed as a weakness by MHT (4:141–42), but which was the favored rhetorical style of Asia Minor. BDF (§493.3) points to this as an example of climax. In this virtual catalogue, the first member assumes what they have ("in your x"), and the second gives a virtue they are to "furnish" or "supply." The order of virtues does not seem to be significant, although the number seven (including πίστις, "commitment") may indicate a fully rounded virtuous character.

ἐν τῇ πίστει. Association.

ὑμῶν. Subjective genitive.

τὴν ἀρετήν. Accusative direct object of ἐπιχορηγήσατε. This Hellenistic term, which is rare in the NT (Phil 4:8; 1 Pet 2:9 in a quotation; three times in 2 Pet 1:3, 5), refers to "uncommon character worthy of praise, *excellence of character, exceptional civic virtue*," and thus the phrase may be translated "*bring the finest character to your commitment*" (BDAG, 130.1).

ἐν ... τῇ ἀρετῇ. Association.

τὴν γνῶσιν. Accusative direct object of an implied ἐπιχορηγήσατε.

1:6 ἐν δὲ τῇ γνώσει τὴν ἐγκράτειαν, ἐν δὲ τῇ ἐγκρατείᾳ τὴν ὑπομονήν, ἐν δὲ τῇ ὑπομονῇ τὴν εὐσέβειαν,

ἐν... τῇ γνώσει. Association.

τὴν ἐγκράτειαν. Accusative direct object of an implied ἐπιχορηγήσατε. While ἐγκράτεια was a common Hellenistic virtue, this term, which refers to "restraint of one's emotions, impulses, or desires, *self-control*" (BDAG, 274), is rare in the NT (Acts 24:25; Gal 5:23; twice in 2 Pet 1:6). Three of these are in virtue catalogues (Gal 5:23 and 2 Pet 1:6) and it also appears in such a catalogue in *1 Clem.* 35.2; 62.2; 64, in the latter two with a synonym of ὑπομονή.

ἐν... τῇ ἐγκρατείᾳ. Association.

τὴν ὑπομονήν. Accusative direct object of an implied ἐπιχορηγήσατε. In contrast to ἐγκράτεια, ὑπομονή ("patient endurance") was a cardinal Christian virtue (it occurs 32 times in 26 different verses in the NT), found mostly in Paul (Rom, 2 Cor, 2 Thess and the Pastorals), Hebrews, James, and Revelation. The saying on patient endurance found in both Jas 1:2-3 and Rom 5:3-5 is of particular significance, as well as its absence from 1 Peter, even in the parallel to the Jas 1:2-3 passage (1 Pet 1:6-7), indicating both its importance as a virtue and the interest in 1 Peter on persecution as refining rather than as something to be endured.

ἐν... τῇ ὑπομονῇ. Association.

τὴν εὐσέβειαν. Accusative direct object of an implied ἐπιχορηγήσατε. Other than in Acts 3:12, εὐσέβεια is found only in the Pastorals (10 times, concentrated in 1 Tim) and 2 Peter (4 times in two passages, here and in 3:11). A common classical and Hellenistic Greek virtue, in the LXX and Christian literature it means "awesome respect accorded to God, *devoutness, piety, godliness*" (BDAG, 412).

1:7 ἐν δὲ τῇ εὐσεβείᾳ τὴν φιλαδελφίαν, ἐν δὲ τῇ φιλαδελφίᾳ τὴν ἀγάπην.

ἐν... τῇ εὐσεβείᾳ. Association.

τὴν φιλαδελφίαν. Accusative direct object of an implied ἐπιχορηγήσατε. The term φιλαδελφία occurs in Hellenistic Greek literature for love of one's blood brother or sister (BDAG, 1055), but is relatively rare in the NT (Rom 12:10; 1 Thess 4:9; Heb 13:1; 1 Pet 1:22; and twice here). In all Christian usages the virtue is presenting the fictive family of believers in Jesus as one's "true" family, which takes precedence over blood family (cf. Mark 3:31-35).

ἐν ... τῇ φιλαδελφίᾳ. Association.

τὴν ἀγάπην. Accusative direct object of an implied ἐπιχορηγήσατε.

1:8 ταῦτα γὰρ ὑμῖν ὑπάρχοντα καὶ πλεονάζοντα οὐκ ἀργοὺς οὐδὲ ἀκάρπους καθίστησιν εἰς τὴν τοῦ κυρίου ἡμῶν Ἰησοῦ Χριστοῦ ἐπίγνωσιν·

ταῦτα ... ὑμῖν ὑπάρχοντα καὶ πλεονάζοντα. Nominative absolute participial phrase (Wallace, 654). The nominative plural ταῦτα is modified by both ὑπάρχοντα and πλεονάζοντα and together they present the situation that is the logical subject of the verb καθίστησιν. But they are all plurals and the verb is singular, so the connection is logical rather than strictly grammatical, although neuter plural subjects are often viewed as a whole and thus take a singular verb (Zerwick, 717).

ταῦτα. Nominative subject of ὑπάρχοντα. Lit. "these things being to you."

ὑμῖν. Dative of possession (Wallace, 151; BDF §189).

ὑπάρχοντα. Pres act ptc neut nom pl ὑπάρχω (condition). Here, ὑπάρχω is used in a dative of possession construction (MHT, 3:240). Codex A and a few later manuscripts have πάροντα (from πάρειμι, "are present"), perhaps because this sounded similar to ὑπάρχοντα or their eyes skipped down to πάρεστιν in the following verse.

πλεονάζοντα. Pres act ptc neut nom pl πλεονάζω (condition).

ἀργοὺς. Complement in an object-complement double accusative construction (see further below on καθίστησιν). The adjective appears only eight times in the NT and means "idle," "not working," "useless."

ἀκάρπους. Complement in an object-complement double accusative construction (see further below on καθίστησιν). This and the previous adjective both begin with the alpha privative, giving a pleasing rhetorical effect.

καθίστησιν. Pres act ind 3rd sg καθίστημι. Here, it is used with a double accusative construction: "to make someone something" or "to cause to be in a certain state" (Friberg, 211). The accusative direct object (ὑμᾶς) is left implicit.
εἰς τὴν ... ἐπίγνωσιν. Respect or result (see Davids 2006, 185).
τοῦ κυρίου. Objective genitive.
ἡμῶν. Genitive of subordination.
Ἰησοῦ Χριστοῦ. Genitive in apposition to τοῦ κυρίου. See also Jude 1 on Χριστοῦ.

1:9 ᾧ γὰρ μὴ πάρεστιν ταῦτα, τυφλός ἐστιν μυωπάζων, λήθην λαβὼν τοῦ καθαρισμοῦ τῶν πάλαι αὐτοῦ ἁμαρτιῶν.

ᾧ ... μὴ πάρεστιν ταῦτα. The relative clause functions as the grammatical subject of ἐστιν.
ᾧ. Dative of location or possession ("For the one who does not possess these things ...").
πάρεστιν. Pres act ind 3rd sg πάρειμι.
ταῦτα. Nominative plural (collective) subject of πάρεστιν.
τυφλός. Predicate adjective.
ἐστιν. Pres act ind 3rd sg εἰμί.
μυωπάζων. Pres act ptc masc nom sg μυωπάζω (predicate participle in apposition to τυφλός). The verb is a NT *hapax legomenon* meaning "being nearsighted" or "seeing poorly" (Friberg, 267).
λήθην λαβών. Lit. "taking forgetfulness," a periphrastic expression meaning "being forgetful" (BDAG, 584–85.10.c).
λήθην. Accusative direct object of λαβών.
λαβών. Aor act ptc masc nom sg λαμβάνω. The participle could be causal ("he is blind [and] nearsighted, because he has forgotten that he has been cleansed from his past sins") or another appositional predicate participle ("he is blind, nearsighted, [and] has forgotten that he has been cleansed from his past sins").
τοῦ καθαρισμοῦ. Objective genitive, modifying λήθην.
τῶν ... ἁμαρτιῶν. Objective genitive, modifying καθαρισμοῦ. Some manuscripts (ℵ A K Ψ *pc*) use the less common ἁμαρτημάτων, which occurs four other times in the NT. The NA[27]/UBS[4] text is supported by 𝔓[72] B C 𝔐 *al*.
αὐτοῦ. Subjective genitive.

1:10 διὸ μᾶλλον, ἀδελφοί, σπουδάσατε βεβαίαν ὑμῶν τὴν κλῆσιν καὶ ἐκλογὴν ποιεῖσθαι· ταῦτα γὰρ ποιοῦντες οὐ μὴ πταίσητέ ποτε.

A pair of sentences concludes the paragraph that forms the letter opening. The phrase διὸ μᾶλλον signals a conclusion (in this case imperatival) and the οὕτως γὰρ of the following sentence (v. 11) introduces the reason that the action of the imperative is appropriate. Scribes of some important manuscripts (ℵ A *pm*) apparently did not find this sentence clear and thus restructured it: σπουδάσατε ἵνα διὰ τῶν καλῶν ἔργων βεβαίαν ... ποιῆσθε (or ποιεῖσθε). The NA²⁷/UBS⁴ text is supported by 𝔓⁷² B C 𝔐 *pm*.

διὸ μᾶλλον. The inferential conjunction διὸ is common enough in the NT (53 times; three times in 2 Peter and always in material not taken from Jude), but only here is it combined with the comparative adverb μᾶλλον (also common on its own: 81 times in the NT, but only here in 2 Peter), suggesting that this conclusion is in contrast to the negative situation portrayed in the previous sentence.

ἀδελφοί. Vocative.

σπουδάσατε. Aor act impv 2nd pl σπουδάζω. The *inclusio* formed with verse 5 (σπουδὴν) gives the reader another signal that a unit is ending (see also v. 11 on ἐπιχορηγηθήσεται). This verb is characteristic of 2 Peter (3 of 11 times in the NT, four of the others being in the Pastorals) and associated with his use of διὸ.

βεβαίαν. Complement in an object-complement double accusative construction.

ὑμῶν. Objective genitive.

τὴν κλῆσιν καὶ ἐκλογὴν. Accusative direct object of ποιεῖσθαι.

ποιεῖσθαι. Pres mid inf ποιέω (complementary). Since Codex A and ℵ have turned this into a purpose clause by adding ἵνα διὰ τῶν καλῶν ἔργων before βεβαίαν, they must accordingly change the infinitive to ποιῆσθε (pres mid subj 2nd pl).

ταῦτα. Accusative direct object of ποιοῦντες.

ποιοῦντες. Pres act ptc masc nom pl ποιέω (condition or means).

οὐ μὴ ... ποτε. The combination of οὐ μὴ with ποτε produces a very emphatic statement.

πταίσητε. Aor act subj 2nd pl πταίω. The subjunctive is used with οὐ μὴ, which expresses emphatic negation. This verb, meaning "to lose one's footing, stumble, trip" and metaphorically "to experience disaster, be ruined, be lost" (BDAG, 894), occurs only five times in the NT (also Rom 11:11; Jas 2:10; twice in 3:2). In the NT, it always refers to stumbling or being lost with respect to the faith.

1:11 οὕτως γὰρ πλουσίως ἐπιχορηγηθήσεται ὑμῖν ἡ εἴσοδος εἰς τὴν αἰώνιον βασιλείαν τοῦ κυρίου ἡμῶν καὶ σωτῆρος Ἰησοῦ Χριστοῦ.

οὕτως. Manner (BDAG, 742.1.b).
ἐπιχορηγηθήσεται. Fut pass ind 3rd sg ἐπιχορηγέω. The use of this same verb in verse 5 helps form an *inclusio* with that verse (see also v. 10 on σπουδάσατε).
ὑμῖν. Dative of advantage or dative indirect object of ἐπιχορηγηθήσεται.
ἡ εἴσοδος. Nominative subject of ἐπιχορηγηθήσεται.
εἰς τὴν αἰώνιον βασιλείαν. Locative.
τοῦ κυρίου ... καὶ σωτῆρος. Subjective genitive. The Granville-Sharp Rule applies here since there are two nouns linked by καί, neither of which are proper names, with a single article (see also v. 2). Ἰησοῦ Χριστοῦ is in apposition to the single person τοῦ κυρίου ἡμῶν καὶ σωτῆρος (see also 1:1 on τοῦ θεοῦ ἡμῶν καὶ σωτῆρος Ἰησοῦ Χριστοῦ).
ἡμῶν. Genitive of subordination.
Ἰησοῦ Χριστοῦ. Genitive in apposition to τοῦ κυρίου ... καὶ σωτῆρος. See also Jude 1 on Χριστοῦ.

2 Peter 1:12-15

[12]Therefore, I intend to always remind you concerning these things, even though (you) know (them) and are established in the truth present (with you). [13]And I consider it right, so long as I am in this "tent," to refresh your memory, [14]since I know that the "putting aside" of my "tent" is imminent, just as our Lord Jesus the Anointed One has also made clear to me. [15]Morever, I will make

every effort to have you (able) at any time to recall these things after my departure.

This paragraph forms the purpose statement of the letter.

1:12 Διὸ μελλήσω ἀεὶ ὑμᾶς ὑπομιμνῄσκειν περὶ τούτων καίπερ εἰδότας καὶ ἐστηριγμένους ἐν τῇ παρούσῃ ἀληθείᾳ.

Indicating the start of a new paragraph that builds on the previous one by the inferential conjunction διὸ, 2 Peter shifts to the *topos* of reminder/remembrance, giving a socially appropriate defense of his opening paragraph, the contents of which the readers should already "know." There is some textual uncertainty, for 𝔓⁷² and a few other manuscripts read δι' οὐ μελλήσω, apparently reading διὸ as a conflation of δι' οὐ, which in turn could be the basis for the reading in 𝔐 and some of the versions: διὸ οὐκ ἀμελήσω ("I will not be negligent," NKJV). The NA²⁷/UBS⁴ text is supported by ℵ A B C *pc*.

μελλήσω. Fut act ind 1st sg μέλλω. The verb μέλλω is used with an infinitive to form a periphrastic future expression. The future perspective is that of the author when writing.

ἀεὶ. The temporal adverb is rare in the New Testament, occurring 8 times, 2 of which are in quotations and two of which are textually disputed (BDF §105).

ὑμᾶς. Accusative direct object of ὑπομιμνῄσκειν.

ὑπομιμνῄσκειν. Pres act inf ὑπομιμνῄσκω (complementary).

περὶ τούτων. Reference.

καίπερ. Concessive conjunction meaning "even though," "but nevertheless" (Friberg, 212), which reduces ambiguity and fixes the meaning of the participle (MHT, 1:230; BDF §425).

εἰδότας. Prf act ptc masc acc pl οἶδα (concessive with καίπερ; cf. MHT, 3:153). This verb (the perfect form of the obsolete εἴδω) is normally in the perfect tense; many have read it as a perfect with a present force (see Wallace, 580), although many grammarians now argue that the stative aspect of the perfect is enough to explain this verb (see Porter, 39–40). The number and case is taken from ὑμᾶς.

ἐστηριγμένους. Prf pass ptc masc acc pl στηρίζω (concessive with καίπερ). See also above on εἰδότας.

ἐν τῇ ... ἀληθείᾳ. Reference or sphere.

παρούσῃ. Pres act ptc fem dat sg πάρειμι (attributive). The whole PP could indicate "in the truth present (among you)" (see BDAG, 773.1.a) or "in the truth that has come to you" (see BDAG, 773.1.b; NRSV).

1:13 δίκαιον δὲ ἡγοῦμαι, ἐφ' ὅσον εἰμὶ ἐν τούτῳ τῷ σκηνώματι, διεγείρειν ὑμᾶς ἐν ὑπομνήσει,

δίκαιον ... ἡγοῦμαι. An idiom for considering something right, i.e., a just cause (BDAG, 247.2, s.v. δίκαιος).

δίκαιον. Complement in an object-complement double accusative construction, with the direct object "it" implied (Culy 2009, 100–101).

ἡγοῦμαι. Pres mid ind 1st sg ἡγέομαι.

ἐφ' ὅσον. Introduces a temporal adverbial clause, with the correlative adjective "used substantivally with measurements of space, time, number, size, degree in the sense *in such an amount as*" (Friberg, 286).

εἰμὶ. Pres act ind 1st sg εἰμί.

ἐν τούτῳ τῷ σκηνώματι. Locative. The term σκήνωμα ("tent" or "tentlike dwelling") is used in Acts 7:26 of the temple and in this verse and the following verse figuratively of the body (BDAG, 929; Friberg, 350). The far more common cognates are σκηνή and σκῆνος. The former also occurs in Acts 7 and is most common in Hebrews, but it is never used figuratively of the body. The latter is used figuratively by Paul in 2 Cor 5:1, 4 to refer to the body. Also worth noting is the fact that the cognate verb σκηνόω is used figuratively once, of the incarnation of the word (John 1:14).

διεγείρειν ὑμᾶς ἐν ὑπομνήσει. Lit. "to awaken you in remembrance."

διεγείρειν. Pres act inf διεγείρω (complementary with ἡγοῦμαι).

ὑμᾶς. Accusative direct object of διεγείρειν.

ἐν ὑπομνήσει. Instrumental ("to awaken you by reminding") or reference/respect ("to awaken you with reference to remembrance"). The noun indicates "the act of calling to someone's mind, *reminding*" or "the act of remembering, *remembrance*" (BDAG, 1039). It occurs only three times in the NT (see also

3:1 and 2 Tim 1:5). Both occurrences in 2 Peter are found in essentially the same construction. Stylistically, this construction enables the author to avoid repeating the ὑπομιμνῄσκειν of the previous verse.

1:14 εἰδὼς ὅτι ταχινή ἐστιν ἡ ἀπόθεσις τοῦ σκηνώματός μου καθὼς καὶ ὁ κύριος ἡμῶν Ἰησοῦς Χριστὸς ἐδήλωσέν μοι,

εἰδὼς. Prf act ptc masc nom sg οἶδα (causal).
ὅτι. Introduces the clausal complement of εἰδὼς. A ὅτι clause normally follows a verb of thinking, judging, or believing to give the content of the thought process (Friberg, 287).
ταχινή. Predicate adjective. Only here and in 2:1 in the NT: "pert. to taking place without delay" (BDAG, 992.2).
ἐστιν. Pres act ind 3rd sg εἰμί.
ἡ ἀπόθεσις. Nominative subject of ἐστιν. This term occurs only twice in the NT (also 1 Pet 3:21) and is not found in the LXX or the Apostolic Fathers. It means "removal, getting rid of" (BDAG, 110), and is derived from τίθημι.
τοῦ σκηνώματός. Objective genitive.
μου. Possessive genitive.
καθὼς. Introduces a comparison clause (see BDAG, 493.1).
ὁ κύριος. Nominative subject of ἐδήλωσέν.
ἡμῶν. Genitive of subordination.
Ἰησοῦς Χριστὸς. Genitive in apposition to ὁ κύριος. See also Jude 1 on Χριστοῦ.
ἐδήλωσέν. Aor act ind 3rd sg δηλόω.
μοι. Dative indirect object of ἐδήλωσέν.

1:15 σπουδάσω δὲ καὶ ἑκάστοτε ἔχειν ὑμᾶς μετὰ τὴν ἐμὴν ἔξοδον τὴν τούτων μνήμην ποιεῖσθαι.

σπουδάσω. Fut act ind 1st sg σπουδάζω. The future tense (A B C P Ψ 𝔐) apparently sounded so much like the present that it was shifted to the more usual present in 𝔓⁷² and ℵ. The NA²⁷/UBS⁴ text is the slightly more difficult reading. There is no future middle form for this verb in Koine Greek (BDF §77), so that would not have been a possible choice for either our author or a copyist.

The use of σπουδάσω and μνήμην in this verse are cited by MHT (4:142) as examples of the grandiose, or Asian style.

ἑκάστοτε. Temporal adverb, a NT *hapax legomenon*, preferred by Atticists and meaning "at any time" or "always" (BDAG, 298). Here, it likely modifies ἔχειν rather than σπουδάσω, both because of phrasing (the δὲ καὶ making a separation) and because it fits with the imperfective aspect of ἔχειν.

ἔχειν. Pres act inf ἔχω (complementary with σπουδάσω). Here, ἔχω means "be in a position to do something" (BDAG, 421.5), and itself takes a complementary infinitive (ποιεῖσθαι).

ὑμᾶς. Accusative subject of ἔχειν.

μετὰ τὴν ἐμὴν ἔξοδον. Temporal. While in Second Temple literature, including the LXX, ἔξοδος can mean "departure," and in particular the departure of Israel from Egypt (e.g., Heb 11:22), it was also used as a euphemism for death, i.e., "departure from among the living," as here (see also Wis 3:2; 7:6; Luke 9:3; BDAG, 350.2). In only appears three times in the NT.

τὴν ... μνήμην. Accusative object of ποιεῖσθαι. The noun μνήμη is a NT *hapax legomenon* derived from the the LXX (MHT, 4:143), as are 24 of 2 Peter's 55 NT *hapax legomena*. This is the third different way in four verses that 2 Peter refers to memory, demonstrating good stylistic variety.

τούτων. Objective genitive. BDF (§284.3) calls this a possessive genitive and lists it as a use of the emphatic οὗτος in the attributive position.

ποιεῖσθαι. Pres mid inf ποιέω (complementary with ἔχειν).

2 Peter 1:16-21

[16]For we did not make known to you the powerful Parousia of our Lord, Jesus the Anointed One, by following cleverly thought up tales, but by becoming eyewitnesses of his majesty. [17]For when he received honor and glory from Father God, and a voice came to him from the majestic glory such as this, "This is my beloved Son, with whom I am pleased," [18]we also heard this voice as it came from heaven, while we were with him on the holy mountain. [19]And we have the prophetic word confirmed, to which you do well to pay attention as to a light shining in a dark place, until the day

dawns and the morning star rises in your hearts, ²⁰since you know this, first of all, that every prophecy of Scripture did not come into being by (the prophet's) own interpretation. ²¹For prophecy was never brought about by human will, but people spoke from God as they were carried by the Holy Spirit.

1:16 Οὐ γὰρ σεσοφισμένοις μύθοις ἐξακολουθήσαντες ἐγνωρίσαμεν ὑμῖν τὴν τοῦ κυρίου ἡμῶν Ἰησοῦ Χριστοῦ δύναμιν καὶ παρουσίαν ἀλλ᾽ ἐπόπται γενηθέντες τῆς ἐκείνου μεγαλειότητος.

Οὐ. This is one of the few cases in the NT where the usual rule that μή negates the participle is set aside (MHT, 1:231).

γὰρ. Introduces a paragraph that gives the reason why it is so important to keep "these things" in memory: These things are based on eyewitness testimony to the enthronization of Jesus (Davids 2006, 202), which confirmed the prophetic word.

σεσοφισμένοις. Prf pass ptc masc dat pl σοφίζω (attributive). This verb appears in the NT only here and in 2 Tim 3:15. Here, it means "to be skilled in formulating or creating something in an artful manner, frequently with implication of self-serving cleverness" (BDAG, 935.2).

μύθοις. Dative complement of ἐξακολουθήσαντες. The term appears in the NT only in the Pastorals (four times) and here and refers to a "tale, story, legend, myth" (BDAG, 660).

ἐξακολουθήσαντες. Aor act ptc masc nom pl ἐξακολουθέω (means). The verb is used in the NT only here and twice in 2:2. Here, the sense is "to accept as authoritative determiner of thought or action" (BDAG, 344.1).

ἐγνωρίσαμεν. Aor act ind 1st pl γνωρίζω. This is the causative usage of the verb ("to cause information to become known"; so BDAG, 203.1), not the possessive usage ("to have information" or "to be knowledgeable about"; see BDAG, 203.2). Note that Wallace (398) believes that this is a clear example of an exclusive "we" in contrast to 3:13, where one has a clear example of an inclusive "we." How inclusive the "we" is will determine the author's relationship to the addressees and to the group that were physical eyewitnesses of the Transfiguration.

ὑμῖν. Dative indirect object of ἐγνωρίσαμεν.

τὴν ... δύναμιν καὶ παρουσίαν. Accusative direct object of ἐγνωρίσαμεν. The pair probably illustrates "the co-ordination of two ideas, one of which is dependent on the other (hendiadys)" (BDF §442.16) and so means "powerful coming," or given that παρουσίαν is probably used technically, "powerful Parousia" (cf. also MHT, 3:235–36). The term παρουσία is often used as a technical term, and so refers to the "coming of a hidden divinity, who makes his presence felt by a revelation of his power" or "a visit of a person of high rank, especially of kings and emperors visiting a province" (BDAG, 780–81). These two meanings "shade off into one another, or even coincide" and so the term in the New Testament usually (at least 20 of 24 occurrences) refers to "Christ, and nearly always [to] his Messianic Advent in glory to judge the world" (BDAG, 781).

τοῦ κυρίου. Subjective genitive.

ἡμῶν. Genitive of subordination.

Ἰησοῦ Χριστοῦ. Genitive in apposition to τοῦ κυρίου. See also Jude 1 on Χριστοῦ.

ἐπόπται. Predicate nominative. A NT *hapax legomenon*: "eyewitnesses."

γενηθέντες. Aor pass ptc masc nom pl γίνομαι (means, contrasting with the parallel ἐξακολουθήσαντες to which it is joined by ἀλλά).

τῆς ... μεγαλειότητος. Objective genitive. This term appears only three times in the NT. In Luke 9:43 and Acts 19:27 it refers to the majesty of a deity.

ἐκείνου. Subjective genitive.

1:17 λαβὼν γὰρ παρὰ θεοῦ πατρὸς τιμὴν καὶ δόξαν φωνῆς ἐνεχθείσης αὐτῷ τοιᾶσδε ὑπὸ τῆς μεγαλοπρεποῦς δόξης· ὁ υἱός μου ὁ ἀγαπητός μου οὗτός ἐστιν εἰς ὃν ἐγὼ εὐδόκησα,

λαβών. Aor act ptc masc nom sg λαμβάνω (temporal).

γάρ. Introduces an elaboration of the content of the eyewitness account, with this verse indicating what happened and the following verse returning to the theme of their being eyewitnesses in an ABA structure.

παρὰ θεοῦ πατρός. Source. While some manuscripts (ℵ C Ψ *pc*) add τοῦ before θεοῦ, making πατρός a genitive in apposition to θεοῦ, here the anarthrous θεοῦ πατρός likely functions as a proper name (MHT, 3:174; BDF §254.1).

τιμὴν καὶ δόξαν. Accusative direct object of λαβών.

φωνῆς. Genitive subject of ἐνεχθείσης.

ἐνεχθείσης. Aor pass ptc fem gen sg φέρω. Genitive absolute, temporal. On the form, see Mounce, 265.

τοιᾶσδε. The demonstrative adjective (fem gen sg τοιόσδε) means "such as this, of this kind" (BDAG, 1009) and is a NT *hapax legomenon*. On the form, see MHT, 2:178; 3:192, n. 1; BDF §64.4.

ὑπὸ τῆς μεγαλοπρεποῦς δόξης. Ultimate agency. The adjective μεγαλοπρεπής is a NT *hapax legomenon* meaning "magnificent, sublime, majestic, impressive" (BDAG, 622). The phrase "majestic glory" is probably a circumlocution for God, who is about to be quoted.

ὁ υἱός μου ὁ ἀγαπητός μου οὗτός ἐστιν. In many manuscripts (ℵ A C Ψ 𝔐 *pm*), this is not surprisingly conformed to Matt 17:5 (οὗτός ἐστιν ὁ υἱός μου ὁ ἀγαπητός), which does not have the second μου, forcing one to read ὁ ἀγαπητός as substantival and nominative in apposition to ὁ υἱός: "This is my Son, my beloved." The NA²⁷/UBS⁴ text (following 𝔓⁷² B) is the more difficult reading.

ὁ υἱός ... ὁ ἀγαπητός. Predicate nominative.

μου ... μου. Genitive of relationship.

ἐστιν. Pres act ind 3rd sg εἰμί.

εἰς ὃν ἐγὼ εὐδόκησα. The relative clause modifies υἱός. On the interchange of ἐν (found in a few later manuscripts of this passage and in Matt 17:5) and εἰς in a metaphorical sense, see BDF §206.2. Normally one would expect ἐν plus a dative of cause here (BDF §196).

ἐγώ. The personal pronoun is used for emphasis with a subject focus (Wallace, 322–23).

εὐδόκησα. Aor act ind 1st sg εὐδοκέω. As Culy, Parsons, and Stigall (119) note with reference to the parallel usage in Luke 3:22, "This is a good example of why some scholars (e.g., Porter, Decker, Campbell) maintain that the aorist tense, like the other tenses, does not explicitly refer to time, though it is used most often to refer to past events (cf. 1:47; 7:35; 15:24). Here, God is simply portrayed as speaking of his pleasure with Jesus as a whole action or simple event by using the aorist tense/perfective aspect (cf. McKay, 27) rather than as a process (imperfective aspect). There is no indication in the context that God's pleasure with Jesus begins at this point, which would require that God also began to be pleased with Jesus at the Transfiguration (see the use of εὐδόκησα in 17:5; contra, e.g., Wallace, 544, and Nolland, 1:164–65, who take this as an ingressive aorist)."

1:18 καὶ ταύτην τὴν φωνὴν ἡμεῖς ἠκούσαμεν ἐξ οὐρανοῦ ἐνεχθεῖσαν σὺν αὐτῷ ὄντες ἐν τῷ ἁγίῳ ὄρει.

The only text-critical issues in this last part of the sentence (vv. 16-18) are attempts to improve the style, perhaps unconscious to the scribe, with some manuscripts adding articles: ἐκ τοῦ οὐρανοῦ (ℵ A Ψ *pc*) for ἐξ οὐρανοῦ and τῷ ὄρει τῷ ἁγίῳ (ℵ A Ψ 𝔐 *pc*) for τῷ ἁγίῳ ὄρει. The NA²⁷/UBS⁴ text (𝔓⁷² B C* 33 *pc*) with the genitive phrase coming between the article and the noun is itself an example of the good classical word order often found in 2 Peter (MHT, 4:140).

καὶ ταύτην τὴν φωνὴν ἡμεῖς ἠκούσαμεν ἐξ οὐρανοῦ ἐνεχθεῖσαν. The use of the adverbial καί ("also"), the fronted direct object with a demonstrative modifier, and the explicit subject pronoun to begin this main clause of verses 16-18 all highlight the fact that Peter has come to his focal point in this sub-section.

ταύτην τὴν φωνὴν. Accusative direct object of ἠκούσαμεν. In the NT, there does not appear to be a distinction between the use of ἀκούω with the accusative and ἀκούω with the genitive (see Wallace, 133–34; cf. BDF §173.2; Culy and Parsons 2003, 172–73).

ἡμεῖς. The explicit subject pronoun is emphatic (Wallace, 323).

ἠκούσαμεν. Aor act ind 1st pl ἀκούω.

ἐξ οὐρανοῦ. Source, modifying ἐνεχθεῖσαν.

ἐνεχθεῖσαν. Aor pass ptc fem acc sg φέρω (attributive). The use of the same participle links this verse to verse 17. On the tense of the participle, see MHT, 1:221.

σὺν αὐτῷ. Association.

ὄντες. Pres act ptc masc nom pl εἰμί (temporal).
ἐν τῷ ἁγίῳ ὄρει. Locative.

1:19 καὶ ἔχομεν βεβαιότερον τὸν προφητικὸν λόγον, ᾧ καλῶς ποιεῖτε προσέχοντες ὡς λύχνῳ φαίνοντι ἐν αὐχμηρῷ τόπῳ, ἕως οὗ ἡμέρα διαυγάσῃ καὶ φωσφόρος ἀνατείλῃ ἐν ταῖς καρδίαις ὑμῶν,

The experience of the previous three verses segues into the prophetic word that it confirms in a statement full of imagery.

καί. The conjunction introduces the result of what precedes ("and so"; BDAG, 495.1.b.ζ), which MHT (3:334) calls a consecutive nuance.

ἔχομεν. Pres act ind 1st pl ἔχω.

βεβαιότερον. Complement in an object-complement double accusative construction. This is the comparative form of βέβαιος, which previously appeared in verse 9 (otherwise in the NT it occurs four times in Hebrews and twice in Paul).

τὸν προφητικὸν λόγον. Accusative direct object of ἔχομεν. While terms for prophecy are common enough in the New Testament, προφητικός itself is rare, appearing only here and in Rom 16:26, where it refers to prophetic writings.

ᾧ. Dative complement of προσέχοντες.

ποιεῖτε. Pres act ind 2nd pl ποιέω.

προσέχοντες. Pres act ptc masc nom pl προσέχω. The participle could introduce the means of doing well ("by paying attention to it you do well") or a condition for doing well ("you do well if you pay attention to it"). Or, it could serve as a predicative participle (MHT, 3:159) or supplementary participle with a verb of being or doing (BDF §414. 5): "to which you do well to pay attention."

ὡς. Introduces a comparison between λύχνῳ and ᾧ (τὸν προφητικὸν λόγον).

λύχνῳ. Dative complement of an implied form of προσέχω.

φαίνοντι. Pres act ptc masc dat sg φαίνω (attributive).

ἐν αὐχμηρῷ τόπῳ. Locative.

ἕως οὗ. The temporal adverbial phrase ἕως οὗ is not followed by ἄν even though the subjunctive is used (BDF §383).

ἡμέρα. Nominative subject of διαυγάσῃ. Codex ℵ and a few later manuscripts read ἡ ἡμέρα, perhaps due to dittography or to scribes thinking of a specific day.

διαυγάσῃ. Aor act subj 3rd sg διαυγάζω. Subjunctive in an indefinite temporal clause. The verb is a NT *hapax legomenon* meaning "shine through" (BDAG, 238.1), though it occurs in a variant reading at 2 Cor 4:4.

φωσφόρος. Nominative subject of ἀνατείλῃ. BDAG (1073) notes that this NT *hapax legomenon* likely refers to the "morning star."

ἀνατείλῃ. Aor act subj 3rd sg ἀνατέλλω. Subjunctive in an indefinite temporal clause.

1:20 τοῦτο πρῶτον γινώσκοντες ὅτι πᾶσα προφητεία γραφῆς ἰδίας ἐπιλύσεως οὐ γίνεται·

τοῦτο. Accusative direct object of γινώσκοντες.

πρῶτον. Here, the adverbial form of πρῶτος is a marker of degree: "in the first place, above all, especially" (BDAG, 894.2.b).

γινώσκοντες. Pres act ptc masc nom pl γινώσκω (causal).

ὅτι. Introduces a clause that is epexegetical to τοῦτο.

πᾶσα . . . οὐ. While some have viewed this construction as a Hebraism (MHT, 3:196), BDF (§302) points out that this is the less harsh form of such a construction and MHT admits that the construction does occur in non-biblical Greek, so it is the frequency of the construction rather than its absolute use that may show the influence of the LXX.

πᾶσα προφητεία. Nominative subject of γίνεται. This may be read as indicating the class as a whole ("all prophecy") or distributively ("every prophecy"). With a form of πᾶς the presence or absence of the article is not significant (Wallace, 253).

γραφῆς. Genitive of source. Interestingly, 𝔓[72] reads προφητεία καὶ γραφή, which indicates that that scribe apparently thought of the two as separate categories.

ἰδίας ἐπιλύσεως. Genitive of source. The term ἐπίλυσις is a NT *hapax legomenon*, which does not occur in the LXX either, although it does appear in Aquila's version of Gen 40:8. It is frequently used for the interpretation of the parables in Hermas, *Sim.* and may be defined as "the act or process of explaining" (BDAG, 375). The phrase ἰδίας ἐπιλύσεως thus means "its own interpretation," but it is not clear whether this is the interpretation that the prophet gives to his visionary experience or the interpretation that a reader gives to the prophecy.

γίνεται. Pres mid ind 3rd sg γίνομαι.

1:21 οὐ γὰρ θελήματι ἀνθρώπου ἠνέχθη προφητεία ποτέ, ἀλλὰ ὑπὸ πνεύματος ἁγίου φερόμενοι ἐλάλησαν ἀπὸ θεοῦ ἄνθρωποι.

οὐ . . . ποτέ. The clause makes a black and white statement with a strengthened negative (BDF §431.2). 𝔓⁷² and a very few other manuscripts have ἡ προφητεία (a doubling of the η at the end of ἠνέχθη, unless the scribe was thinking about the prophecy referred to in 1:19), but the majority of the manuscript tradition agrees that the text is stating a general principle.

γὰρ. The paragraph concludes with the reason (γὰρ) that prophecy is not characterized by "its own interpretation," with the first clause giving the negative reason (οὐ . . . ποτέ) and the second clause the contrasting (ἀλλὰ) positive reason.

θελήματι. Dative of instrument.

ἀνθρώπου. Subjective genitive.

ἠνέχθη. Aor pass ind 3rd sg φέρω.

προφητεία. Nominative subject of ἠνέχθη.

ὑπὸ πνεύματος ἁγίου. Ultimate agency.

φερόμενοι. Pres pass ptc masc nom pl φέρω (temporal).

ἐλάλησαν. Aor act ind 3rd pl λαλέω.

ἀπὸ θεοῦ. The NA²⁷/UBS⁴ text has strong support (𝔓⁷² B P *al*), but many manuscripts (ℵ A Ψ 𝔐 *al*) read ἅγιοι (τοῦ) θεοῦ ἄνθρωποι. It seems most reasonable to conclude that the preceding ἁγίου and the more straightforward grammar of "holy people of God" have produced the variant reading. Although Wallace (433) cites this passage as an example of agency, the textual variant suggests that early scribes may have read ἀπό as introducing source here.

ἄνθρωποι. Nominative subject of ἐλάλησαν.

2 Peter 2:1-3

¹And there were also false prophets among the people, as there will also be false teachers among you, who will introduce destructive opinions, even denying the Owner who purchased them, quickly bringing upon themselves destruction. ²And many will follow them with respect to their self-abandonment, on account of whom the way of truth will be slandered, ³and they, whose condemnation has not been idle for a long time and whose destruction does not doze off, will exploit you by their deceptive words due to (their) greed.

While the chapter break seems to separate chapter 2 sharply from chapter 1, 2 Peter segues smoothly into this new paragraph, where he begins drawing heavily on Jude. The δὲ marks disjunction, not a sharp disjunction, but a step forward in the argument, and the vocabulary of prophets/prophecy continues. Chapter 1 ends with the importance of prophecy from God through the men God uses and chapter 2 starts with the ancient false prophets and then moves smoothly to the comparable false teachers of the present, who, far from bringing light in a dark place and pointing to the dawning day, bring destruction.

2:1 Ἐγένοντο δὲ καὶ ψευδοπροφῆται ἐν τῷ λαῷ, ὡς καὶ ἐν ὑμῖν ἔσονται ψευδοδιδάσκαλοι, οἵτινες παρεισάξουσιν αἱρέσεις ἀπωλείας καὶ τὸν ἀγοράσαντα αὐτοὺς δεσπότην ἀρνούμενοι. ἐπάγοντες ἑαυτοῖς ταχινὴν ἀπώλειαν,

Structurally, this verse introducing the false teachers is one complex sentence and the start of a second. The first sentence, linked to the preceding paragraph by δὲ καὶ, consists of two independent clauses coordinated by ὡς καὶ in a verb + subject + location and then location + verb + subject structure that makes the parallel very clear.

Ἐγένοντο. Aor mid ind 3rd pl γίνομαι.

ψευδοπροφῆται. Nominative subject of Ἐγένοντο. While ψευδοπροφήτης appears 11 times in the NT (especially in Matthew and Revelation, never in Paul, and only here and 1 John 4:1 in the

Catholic Epistles), ψευδοδιδάσκαλος is a NT *hapax legomenon* used to pick up the earlier term in a different context. They are also examples of word formation in which the second element governs the first (BDF §119.5).

ἐν τῷ λαῷ. Association.

ἔσονται. Fut mid ind 3rd pl εἰμί. The force of the future tense is debatable, as is also the case in the following verse. They appear to be predictive futures (so Wallace, 568, for v. 2), but it becomes clear later that these false teachers already exist, since their activities are described in some detail. The future is future in terms of the predictive stance of the author (between the false prophets and the false teachers), not necessarily in terms of the time of writing of the letter.

παρεισάξουσιν. Fut act ind 3rd pl παρεισάγω. A NT *hapax legomenon* meaning "to bring in something that becomes an addition to something" (BDAG, 774).

αἱρέσεις. Accusative direct object of παρεισάξουσιν. This term appears nine times in the NT and means either "a group that holds tenets distinctive to it, *sect, party, school, faction*" (BDAG, 27.1; e.g., Sadducees, Acts 5:17; Pharisees, Acts 15:5; Nazareans/Christians, Acts 24:5, 14) or, as here, "that which distinguishes a group's thinking, *opinion, dogma*" (BDAG, 28.2). Despite the derivation of the English term "heresy" from this term, the word is not in itself negative in the first century (see, e.g., Acts 26:5; 28:22), although parties within the Jesus movement were frowned upon (1 Cor 11:19; Gal 5:20). What makes the opinions, teaching or dogma negative here is the genitive modifier.

ἀπωλείας. Attributive genitive or perhaps genitive of destination (see Wallace, 100–101). These are not just new opinions that are being introduced, but "destructive opinions" or "opinions that lead to destruction."

καί. Adverbial: "even"; or possibly explicative: "namely, denying" (BDAG, 495.c).

τὸν ἀγοράσαντα. Aor act ptc masc ἀγοράζω (attributive).

αὐτούς. Accusative direct object of ἀγοράσαντα.

δεσπότην. Accusative direct object of ἀρνούμενοι. Borrowed from Jude 4, this term appears elsewhere only in Luke's writings, the Pastoral Epistles, 1 Pet 2:18, and Rev 6:10. It means "one who has legal control and authority over persons, such as subjects or slaves, *lord, master*" (BDAG, 220).

ἀρνούμενοι. Pres mid ptc masc nom pl ἀρνέομαι (result: "who will introduce destructive opinions with the result that they even deny the Master," or attendant circumstance: "who will introduce destructive opinions and even deny the Master").

ἐπάγοντες . . . ἀπώλειαν. The repetition of a form of ἀπώλεια (ἀπώλειαν) from earlier in the verse (ἀπωλείας) forms an *inclusio* with the earlier part of the description of the false teachers. Depending on whether one views this as starting a new topic (the corruption and destruction of the false teachers in vv. 2-3) as NA[27] does or finishing off the previous sentence with a comment about the results of denying the Lord/Master who purchased them as NTGECM does, one either punctuates this with a comma or a period.

ἐπάγοντες. Pres act ptc masc nom pl ἐπάγω (if read as concluding the previous sentence, result; so Wallace, 639; if read as beginning the following sentence, concession).

ἑαυτοῖς. Dative complement of ἐπάγοντες or dative of disadvantage. With the ἐπι- prefix, the verb seems to take a dative complement, though it can also take a direct object as in verse 5.

ταχινὴν ἀπώλειαν. Accusative direct object of ἐπάγοντες. On the derivation of the adjective ταχινός from the noun τάχα, see BDF §113. See also 1:14 on ταχινή.

2:2 καὶ πολλοὶ ἐξακολουθήσουσιν αὐτῶν ταῖς ἀσελγείαις δι᾽ οὓς ἡ ὁδὸς τῆς ἀληθείας βλασφημηθήσεται,

καί. How the καί functions here depends on whether ἐπάγοντες ἑαυτοῖς ταχινὴν ἀπώλειαν goes with the preceding verse or this one. If it goes with verse 1, then καί is a coordinate conjunction. If it goes with this verse, it would be adverbial ("also" or "even").

ἐξακολουθήσουσιν. Fut act ind 3rd pl ἐξακολουθέω (predictive future). This verb appears only in 2 Peter in the NT, although it also occurs in the Wisdom literature of the LXX.

αὐτῶν. Genitive direct object of ἐξακολουθήσουσιν (due to the ἐξ- prefix).

ἀσελγείαις. Dative of reference. This term, which occurs in Jude 4 and is a favorite of 2 Peter (2:2, 7, 18), means "lack of self-constraint which involves one in conduct that violates all bounds of what is socially acceptable, *self-abandonment*" (BDAG, 141). An antonym, ἐγκράτεια, is used in 1:6.

δι' οὕς. Cause.

ἡ ὁδὸς. Nominative subject of βλασφημηθήσεται.

τῆς ἀληθείας. Attributive genitive: "the true way." The phrase ἡ ὁδὸς τῆς ἀληθείας only appears elsewhere in the NT in Mark 12:14 and parallels, so it is not surprising that some manuscripts (ℵ²A *pc*) have ἡ δόξα τῆς ἀληθείας ("the honor of the truth"), for δόξα is an honor term that fits well with both the feminine article and βλασφημηθήσεται, which involves a loss of honor.

βλασφημηθήσεται. Fut pass ind 3rd sg βλασφημέω (predictive future). Wallace (436, n. 92) points to this as an example of a passive verb having "an implicit generic agent."

2:3 καὶ ἐν πλεονεξίᾳ πλαστοῖς λόγοις ὑμᾶς ἐμπορεύσονται, οἷς τὸ κρίμα ἔκπαλαι οὐκ ἀργεῖ καὶ ἡ ἀπώλεια αὐτῶν οὐ νυστάζει.

καί. The conjunction assists in transitioning from the subject of the πολλοί followers of the false teachers back to the actions of the false teachers themselves, i.e., their effect on their followers.

ἐν πλεονεξίᾳ. Cause.

πλαστοῖς λόγοις. Dative of instrument. The adjective is a NT *hapax legomenon* meaning pertaining "to being mentally constructed without a basis in fact, *fabricated, false*" (BDAG, 823).

ὑμᾶς. Accusative direct object of ἐμπορεύσονται.

ἐμπορεύσονται. Fut mid ind 3rd pl ἐμπορεύομαι. While the verb can simply mean "to make gain" or "to do business," as in the only other NT occurrence in Jas 4:13, MHT (2:400) shows that it can also mean "exploit" when it takes a direct object, as here (see also BDF §148.1).

οἷς. Dative of reference (lit. "with reference to whom judgment is not idle") or disadvantage (lit. "against whom judgment is not idle").

τὸ κρίμα ἔκπαλαι. Nominative subject of ἀργεῖ. This temporal adverb, which can mean either "long ago" or "for a long time"

(BDAG, 307), is found in the NT only in 2 Peter (also 3:5) and demonstrates the Koine tendency to prefix prepositions to adverbs (as well as nouns, verbs, and adjectives; see BDF §116.3).

ἀργεῖ. Pres act ind 3rd sg ἀργέω. A NT *hapax legomenon* meaning "be idle, do nothing," except when it is applied to a field and then means "left unplowed and unseeded" (Friberg, 71).

ἡ ἀπώλεια. Nominative subject of νυστάζει.

αὐτῶν. Objective genitive. The pleonastic insertion of the personal pronoun αὐτῶν in this clause is viewed by MHT (3:325) as a Semitism (see also BDF §297).

νυστάζει. Pres act ind 3rd sg νυστάζω. This verb is found twice in the NT (also in Matt 25:5) and means "become drowsy, doze, get sleepy" (Friberg, 274). Here, their destruction is personified as not dozing.

2 Peter 2:4-10a

⁴For if God did not spare the angels who sinned, but held them captive in Tartarus in pits of darkness and handed over (to prison) those being kept for judgment, ⁵and (if) he did not spare the ancient world, but protected seven others and Noah, a preacher of righteousness, when he brought a flood upon the world of the ungodly, ⁶and (if) he condemned the cities of Sodom and Gomorrah to destruction, reducing them to ashes, making (them) an example of what was coming to the impious, ⁷but he delivered a righteous man, Lot, who had been oppressed by the lifestyle in indecency of those disgraceful individuals—⁸for that righteous (man), as he lived among them day after day, tormented his righteous soul by what he saw and heard, by (their) lawless deeds— ⁹(then) the Lord knows (how) to deliver the godly from testing, and (how) to keep the unrighteous, who are being punished, for the day of judgment, ¹⁰especially those who go after flesh according to corrupt desire and who despise lordships.

The previous paragraph ended with the image of unslumbering judgment coming upon the false teachers; this paragraph provides the historical support for that statement and thus starts with a postpositive γάρ. The paragraph is a single first class (real) conditional sentence (Wallace, 694), with the protasis covering the first five verses, consisting of three "if" clauses with a parenthetic explanatory expansion to the final one. The final three verses form the apodosis, the last two of which explain which ἀδίκους in particular are in view in terms of judgment. The first two parts of the protasis are similarly structured: Εἰ A ἀλλὰ B καὶ (Εἰ) C ἀλλὰ D. The third part uses only καί.

2:4 Εἰ γὰρ ὁ θεὸς ἀγγέλων ἁμαρτησάντων οὐκ ἐφείσατο ἀλλὰ σειραῖς ζόφου ταρταρώσας παρέδωκεν εἰς κρίσιν τηρουμένους,

Εἰ. Introduces a first class condition.

γὰρ. Explanatory.

ὁ θεὸς. Nominative subject of ἐφείσατο.

ἀγγέλων. Genitive direct object of ἐφείσατο. This is good classical style (see also MHT, 3:235; BDF §180.5; Acts 20:29; Rom 8:32; 11:21; 1 Cor 7:28; 2 Cor 1:23).

ἁμαρτησάντων. Aor act ptc masc gen pl ἁμαρτάνω (attributive).

ἐφείσατο. Aor mid ind 3rd sg φείδομαι. On the form of the first aorist middle, see BDF §75.

σειραῖς. Dative of instrument ("by ropes or chains") or dative of location (σιροῖς/σειροῖς), depending on one's textual decision. BDF (§23) notes, "The phonetic leveling of ει and ῐ betrays itself by the *rather frequent* confusion in usage in the early Hellenistic period." Accordingly, Codex ℵ reads σιροῖς ("in pits") and A B C 81 use the variant spelling σειροῖς (BDAG, 918). The NA²⁷/UBS⁴ text is supported by 𝔓⁷² K L 33 𝔐 *pm*. The external evidence for the two readings, σειραῖς and σιροῖς/σειροῖς, is thus very evenly divided. See further below.

ζόφου. Genitive of material (with σειραῖς), attributive genitive (with σιροῖς/σειροῖς), or genitive of content (with σιροῖς/σειροῖς), depending on which reading (see above) one selects. The parallel in Jude 6 does refer to "fetters," but then has ὑπὸ ζόφον. The only other use of this term in the NT is in Heb 12:18. The parallel in Jude, a passage in Diogenes Laertius 8.31, and Wis 17:16-17 ("for with one chain of darkness they were bound") all refer to chains or fetters in the underworld, even chains of darkness, although little if any of the vocabulary is common with 2 Peter. This would seem to make σιροῖς/σειροῖς the more difficult reading culturally and the better-supported reading textually (see above). And surely "pits of darkness" both makes sense and fits the descriptions of Tartarus and the prison of the Watchers in *1 Enoch*. Scribes may have changed σιροῖς/σειροῖς to σειραῖς to bring it into semantic conformity with Jude's δεσμοῖς or it may have been a mishearing, as noted in the previous comment. This is one of the few cases where exegetical considerations must be taken into account in making textual decisions.

ταρταρώσας. Aor act ptc masc nom sg ταρταρόω (means or manner). A NT *hapax legomenon* meaning to "*hold captive in Tartarus*" (BDAG, 991).

παρέδωκεν. Aor act ind 3rd sg παραδίδωμι.

εἰς κρίσιν. Purpose or goal.

τηρουμένους. Pres pass ptc masc acc pl τηρέω (substantival). On why this is unlikely to be adverbial, see Culy (2003). The NA²⁷/UBS⁴ text has stronger attestation ($\mathfrak{P}^{72}$ B C 𝔐), while some manuscripts (א A C² Ψ 33 *al*) read κολαζομένους τηρεῖν, with a purpose infinitive and substantival participle: "in order to guard/keep those being punished." The verb κολάζω means to "penalize" or "punish" (BDAG, 554).

2:5 καὶ ἀρχαίου κόσμου οὐκ ἐφείσατο ἀλλὰ ὄγδοον Νῶε δικαιοσύνης κήρυκα ἐφύλαξεν κατακλυσμὸν κόσμῳ ἀσεβῶν ἐπάξας,

While the first part of the protasis, found in 2:4, consisted of the same idea stated first negatively (Εἰ . . . ὁ θεὸς . . . οὐκ ἐφείσατο) and then by way of contrast (ἀλλά) positively (σειραῖς ζόφου ταρταρώσας παρέδωκεν), this second part of the same protasis (the continuing complex Εἰ clause) also consists of contrasting (ἀλλά) ideas. But in this case the first part names those God did not preserve and the second those that he did preserve.

ἀρχαίου κόσμου. Genitive direct object of ἐφείσατο. The article is frequently omitted with κόσμος, as well as with certain other words, in this case to help contrast one world with another, i.e., the ancient one (see BDF §253.4).

ἐφείσατο. Aor mid ind 3rd sg φείδομαι.

ὄγδοον Νῶε. Accusative direct object of ἐφύλαξεν, with the ordinal number ὄγδοος used adverbially in a classical idiom. MHT (1:98) states concerning this phrase, "in 2 Pet we rather expect bookish phrases." The expression means "Noah as the eighth" or, more colloquially, "Noah and seven others" (BDF §248.5).

δικαιοσύνης. Objective genitive.

κήρυκα. Accusative in apposition to Νῶε. The noun κῆρυξ ("preacher," "proclaimer," or "herald") is rare in the NT, appearing only here and twice in the Pastorals.

ἐφύλαξεν. Aor act ind 3rd sg φυλάσσω.

κατακλυσμὸν. Accusative direct object of ἐπάξας. The term appears only four times in the NT (also Matt 24:38, 39 and the parallel account in Luke 17:27 [i.e., Q]) and means "flood, inundation, deluge" (Friberg, 218).

κόσμῳ. Dative complement of ἐπάξας or dative of disadvantage.

ἀσεβῶν. Genitive of content: "the world consisting of the ungodly."

ἐπάξας. Aor act ptc masc nom sg ἐπάγω (temporal). This verb appears in the NT twice in this chapter (vv. 1, 5) and once in Acts 5:28. It takes a double object, an accusative of what is brought (κατακλυσμὸν) and a dative (fitting with the prefix ἐπί-) of whom it is brought upon (κόσμῳ).

2:6 καὶ πόλεις Σοδόμων καὶ Γομόρρας τεφρώσας [καταστροφῇ] κατέκρινεν ὑπόδειγμα μελλόντων ἀσεβέ[σ]ιν τεθεικώς,

πόλεις. Accusative direct object of κατέκρινεν.

Σοδόμων καὶ Γομόρρας. Epexegetical genitive. On the declension of the Semitic city names, see MHT, 2:147; BDF §57.

τεφρώσας. Aor act ptc masc nom sg τεφρόω (means). A NT *hapax legomenon*: "cover with or reduce to ashes" (BDAG, 1001).

[καταστροφῇ]. Dative of instrument or result. BDF (§195.2) and MHT (3:240) both call attention to this "genuinely instrumental" use of the dative. The noun καταστροφή ("overthrow, ruin, destruction") appears only here and in 2 Tim 2:14 in the NT. It is present in the vast majority of manuscripts (ℵ A C² K L Ψ 𝔐 *pm*) but absent in some important ones ($\mathfrak{P}^{75}$ B C* *al*).

κατέκρινεν. Aor act ind 3rd sg κατακρίνω.

ὑπόδειγμα μελλόντων ἀσεβέ[σ]ιν τεθεικώς. Lit. "having set/appointed an example of the things coming to/for the ungodly."

ὑπόδειγμα. Accusative direct object of τεθεικώς or complement in an object-complement double accusative construction with the direct object ("them") implied. This noun appears six times in the NT and refers to "an example of behavior used for purposes of moral instruction, *example, model, pattern*." Here, the example is not of impious behavior, but rather of what will happen to those who live impiously (BDAG, 1037).

μελλόντων. Pres act ptc neut/masc gen pl μέλλω (substantival). The substantival participle is likely neuter and refers to "things to come" (but see also below on ἀσεβέ[σ]ιν). Objective genitive: "he set this forth to exemplify the things to come for the ungodly."

ἀσεβέ[σ]ιν. Dative of advantage. The translation of the phrase depends on how one reads this word. The NA²⁷/UBS⁴ text is supported by 𝔓⁷² B P *al*, but ℵ A C Ψ 𝔐 *pm* read ἀσεβεῖν (pres act inf ἀσεβέω, complementary with μελλόντων; with μελλόντων then being masculine and a genitive of reference): "having set/appointed an example with reference to those who will be impious in the future." The text follows NA²⁷, but the alternative reading is chosen for the text in NTGECM.

τεθεικώς. Prf act ptc masc nom sg τίθημι (result; Wallace, 639).

2:7 καὶ δίκαιον Λὼτ καταπονούμενον ὑπὸ τῆς τῶν ἀθέσμων ἐν ἀσελγείᾳ ἀναστροφῆς ἐρρύσατο·

δίκαιον Λώτ. Accusative direct object of ἐρρύσατο.

καταπονούμενον. Pres pass ptc masc acc sg καταπονέω (attributive). This verb is used in the NT only here and in Acts 7:24 and means "to cause distress through oppressive means" (BDAG, 525). The root verb πονέω is intransitive, but it has been made transitive by the addition of the prefix κατα- (BDF §150).

ὑπὸ τῆς ... ἀναστροφῆς. Ultimate agency.

τῶν ἀθέσμων. Subjective genitive. The term ἄθεσμος means "being unprincipled, *unseemly, disgraceful, lawless*," and is an antonym of δίκαιος (BDAG, 24). Its location here in the classical position is a mark of the good style of 2 Peter (MHT, 3:217; cf. BDF

§271). On the form and origin of the -μος ending, see MHT, 2:353.

ἐν ἀσελγείᾳ. The PP specifies the nature of their conduct. It could be viewed as reference or manner: "by their indecent lifestyle."

ἐρρύσατο. Aor mid ind 3rd sg ῥύομαι. This verb will appear for a second time in verse 9. On the form of the augment, see MHT, 2:193.

2:8 βλέμματι γὰρ καὶ ἀκοῇ ὁ δίκαιος ἐγκατοικῶν ἐν αὐτοῖς ἡμέραν ἐξ ἡμέρας ψυχὴν δικαίαν ἀνόμοις ἔργοις ἐβασάνιζεν·

This verse is 2 Peter's explanatory comment drawn from Second Temple materials (e.g., Wis 10:6; 19:17; Philo, *Mos.* 2.58), justifying what was said about Lot in the previous verse. The grammatical difficulties in this verse for English speakers include (1) the noun pair that starts the verse (βλέμματι . . . καὶ ἀκοῇ; lit. "in seeing and hearing"), since English uses verbal forms to express this idea; (2) the idiom for time (ἡμέραν ἐξ ἡμέρας; lit. "day from day"), where English would use an adjective, "every day," or a temporal preposition, "day after day"; and (3) the unusual (for English speakers) way of referring to Lot's torment (ὁ δίκαιος . . . ψυχὴν δικαίαν ἀνόμοις ἔργοις ἐβασάνιζεν; lit. "the righteous man . . . tormented (his) righteous soul with (their) lawless deeds."

βλέμματι . . . καὶ ἀκοῇ. Dative of instrument. The noun βλέμμα is a NT *hapax legomenon* meaning "look," "glance," "what one sees," "sight" (Friberg, 92).

γὰρ. Explanatory.

ὁ δίκαιος. Nominative subject of ἐβασάνιζεν.

ἐγκατοικῶν. Pres act ptc masc nom sg ἐγκατοικέω (temporal). This verb is a NT *hapax legomenon*: "to live as a resident" (BDAG, 273).

ἐν αὐτοῖς. Association.

ἡμέραν ἐξ ἡμέρας. A classical expression meaning "day after day" (BDF §161.2).

ἡμέραν. Accusative extent of time.

ψυχὴν δικαίαν. Accusative direct object of ἐβασάνιζεν.

ἀνόμοις ἔργοις. Dative of instrument or possibly cause (Green, 260).

ἐβασάνιζεν. Impf act ind 3rd sg βασανίζω.

2:9 οἶδεν κύριος εὐσεβεῖς ἐκ πειρασμοῦ ῥύεσθαι, ἀδίκους δὲ εἰς ἡμέραν κρίσεως κολαζομένους τηρεῖν,

The shift of subject from Lot back to κύριος and the repetition of a form of ῥύομαι signals that the comment about Lot is finished and our author is about to make his summary statement about the three examples cited. This is a very spare, direct statement, as is appropriate for a summary.

οἶδεν. Prf act ind 3rd sg οἶδα. On the verb's tense, see Jude 10 on οἴδασιν. Here, this verb means "to know/understand how, *can, be able*" (BDAG, 694.2).

κύριος. Nominative subject of οἶδεν.

εὐσεβεῖς. Accusative direct object of ῥύεσθαι.

ἐκ πειρασμοῦ. Separation.

ῥύεσθαι. Pres mid inf ῥύομαι (complementary). Some manuscripts ($\mathfrak{P}^{72}$ 69 181 *pc*) have the aorist ῥύσασθαι here.

ἀδίκους. Accusative direct object of τηρεῖν.

εἰς ἡμέραν. Goal or perhaps purpose. The PP introduces that for which the ἀδίκους are being reserved.

κρίσεως. "The day when judgment will take place." MHT (4:143) cites this as an example of the "neglect of the article with a definite noun before a genitive, reflecting the Hebrew construct state."

κολαζομένους. Pres act ptc masc acc pl κολάζω (attributive modifier of ἀδίκους). This verb appears only three times in the NT (also Acts 4:21 and 1 Pet 2:20, in both of which it refers to Christians being punished) but is often used outside of the NT for punishment, including that inflicted by God.

τηρεῖν. Pres act inf τηρέω (complementary with an implied οἶδεν).

2:10a μάλιστα δὲ τοὺς ὀπίσω σαρκὸς ἐν ἐπιθυμίᾳ μιασμοῦ πορευομένους καὶ κυριότητος καταφρονοῦντας.

In this elliptical clause introduced by the adverb μάλιστα ("especially") with δὲ, the two substantival participles (following the Granville-Sharp Rule, these are a single group; see Wallace,

282–83) expand upon the nature of the ἀδίκους referred to in the previous verse and complete the sentence. Note the similarity in vocabulary to Jude 8 (terms in common are in italics): Ὁμοίως μέντοι καὶ οὗτοι ἐνυπνιαζόμενοι *σάρκα μὲν μιαίνουσιν κυριότητα δὲ ἀθετοῦσιν δόξας* (v. 10b) δὲ *βλασφημοῦσιν* (v. 10b).

τοὺς ... πορευομένους. Pres mid ptc masc acc pl πορεύομαι (substantival). Accusative direct object of an implied τηρεῖν.

ὀπίσω σαρκὸς. Here, ὀπίσω is a spatial preposition.

ἐν ἐπιθυμίᾳ μιασμοῦ. The word μιασμός is a NT *hapax legomenon* meaning "defilement" or "corruption" (BDAG, 650). Here, it is used in a construction that MHT (4:143) terms "a double Hebraism" meaning "according to corrupt desire." Commentators have struggled with the meaning of this seemingly ambiguous phrase (MHT, 4:141).

μιασμοῦ. Attributive genitive.

κυριότητος. Genitive complement of καταφρονοῦντας. This term comes from Jude 8 and is found elsewhere in the NT only in Eph 1:21 and Col 1:16. BDAG (579) argues that the singular form here means "the majestic power that the κύριος wields, *ruling power, lordship, dominion*," while in the plural in the Prison Epistles it refers to "a special class of angelic powers, *bearers of the ruling power, dominions*." Both here (i.e., v. 10b) and in Jude 8, however, the despising of "lordship" is expressed in slandering the "glorious ones" (δόξας).

καταφρονοῦντας. Pres act ptc masc acc pl καταφρονέω (substantival). Accusative direct object of an implied τηρεῖν as part of a larger NP (τοὺς ... πορευομένους καὶ ... καταφρονοῦντας).

2 Peter 2:10b-22

10bArrogant! Audacious! They are not afraid to demean the glorious ones, 11whereas angels, although they are greater in terms of strength and power, do not bring against them a demeaning judgment from the Lord. 12But these people—like unreasoning animals that are by nature born for capture and slaughter—who slander that of which they are ignorant, when they are destroyed (physically), they are utterly destroyed (in final judgment), 13when they are harmed by the wage of injustice. They consider indulgence during the daytime (to be) pleasure. They are stains and blemishes, who carouse in their deceptive desires when they feast together with you. ¹⁴They have eyes full of adultery, even (eyes) unceasing with respect to sin. They entice unstable souls. They have hearts trained in greed. Accursed children! ¹⁵Having forsaken the straight way, they wander, following the way of Balaam (son) of Bosor, who loved unjust reward. ¹⁶He received a rebuke for his evildoing: A mute beast of burden, speaking in a human voice prevented the prophet's insanity. ¹⁷These are waterless fountains and mist driven by a storm, for whom the gloom of darkness has been reserved. ¹⁸For, by pronouncing bombastic nonsense they lure by fleshly desires, (that is,) licentiousness, those who are scarcely escaping from those who are living in error, ¹⁹promising them freedom, although they are themselves slaves to corruption—for one has been enslaved to that to which they succumb. ²⁰For if, after escaping the world's shameful deeds by means of the knowledge of our Lord and Savior Jesus the Anointed One, they again succumb, having become entangled, then their last (state) has become worse than their first (state). ²¹For it would have been better for them never to have known the way of righteousness than having known it to turn away from the holy commandments which had been given to them. ²²The true proverb fits them: "The dog returns to its own vomit" and "the washed sow to rolling in the mud."

This passage has a number of tautologies, e.g., the repeated occurrence of the φθορ- root in a single clause and ἀδικούμενοι μισθὸν ἀδικίας. However, it would be more accurate to label them as rhetotorical schemes, especially polyptoton, than Semitisms. See further MHT, 2:420.

2:10b Τολμηταὶ αὐθάδεις, δόξας οὐ τρέμουσιν βλασφημοῦντες,

τολμηταὶ αὐθάδεις. Nominative of exclamation (see Wallace, 59–60), with the second one being in apposition to the first. They are what Porter (85) terms nominal clauses. The noun τολμηρός is a NT *hapax legomenon* meaning "*bold, audacious*" (BDAG, 1010). While cognate terms can be used positively in the NT, here the adjective αὐθάδης ("self-willed, stubborn, arrogant"; BDAG, 150) gives τολμηρός a negative tone, as in the only other appearance of the adjective in the NT (Titus 1:7).

δόξας. Accusative direct object of βλασφημοῦντες.

τρέμουσιν. Pres act ind 3rd pl τρέμω. This verb appears three times in the NT (also Mark 5:33; Luke 8:47) and means "to feel intensely the impact of something transcendent, *tremble, be in awe*" (BDAG, 1014).

βλασφημοῦντες. Pres act ptc masc nom pl βλασφημέω (temporal, "they are not afraid when they demean," though it could perhaps be viewed as supplementary with τρέμουσιν [BDF §415; cf. MHT, 3:160] and thus translated like an infinitive: "they are not afraid to demean").

2:11 ὅπου ἄγγελοι ἰσχύϊ καὶ δυνάμει μείζονες ὄντες οὐ φέρουσιν κατ᾽ αὐτῶν παρὰ κυρίου βλάσφημον κρίσιν.

ὅπου. BDAG (717) refers to its usage in this verse as a "marker of more immediate circumstance or expressing a premise, *where*." BDF (§456.3), on the other hand, takes it as causal. On its relationship to style, see MHT, 4:141. It introduces the dependent clause in the sentence, a negative comparison between "them" and angels.

ἄγγελοι. Nominative subject of φέρουσιν.

ἰσχύϊ καὶ δυνάμει. Dative of reference.

μείζονες. Predicate nominative; comparative form of μέγας.

ὄντες. Pres act ptc masc nom pl εἰμί (concessive).

φέρουσιν. Pres act ind 3rd pl φέρω.

κατ᾽ αὐτῶν. Opposition.

παρὰ κυρίου. Source. Here, a "marker of one who originates or directs" (BDAG, 756.2). Some scribes (A Ψ 33 *pm*) leave this phrase out, perhaps because it does not appear in the parallel in Jude 9. Others supply the detail that it was "before the Lord": παρὰ κυρίῳ (ℵ B C P 𝔐 *al*), with the dative indicating location ("before") or perhaps indirect object ("to"). The oldest voice (𝔓⁷² *pc*), although the minority view, represents the more difficult reading and is followed by the NA[27]/UBS[4]. In this reading, the writer refers to delivering a divine verdict that was, nonetheless, "defaming."

One can understand the other readings arising from this one and the parallel in Jude, but not παρὰ κυρίου arising from the other ones (see Metzger, 633).

βλάσφημον κρίσιν. Accusative direct object of φέρουσιν. The adjective βλάσφημος, meaning "defaming, denigrating, demeaning" (BDAG, 178), is rare in the NT (elsewhere only in Acts 6:11; 1 Tim 1:13; 2 Tim 3:2).

2:12 οὗτοι δὲ ὡς ἄλογα ζῷα γεγεννημένα φυσικὰ εἰς ἅλωσιν καὶ φθορὰν ἐν οἷς ἀγνοοῦσιν βλασφημοῦντες, ἐν τῇ φθορᾷ αὐτῶν καὶ φθαρήσονται

This verse is an edited form of Jude 10 (οὗτοι δὲ ὅσα μὲν οὐκ οἴδασιν βλασφημοῦσιν, ὅσα δὲ φυσικῶς ὡς τὰ ἄλογα ζῷα ἐπίστανται, ἐν τούτοις φθείρονται), which has influenced the textual transmission of our verse (see below).

οὗτοι. Nominative subject of φθαρήσονται.

ὡς. Introduces a comparison.

ἄλογα ζῷα. Nominative subject of an implied φθαρήσονται. Both ἄλογος and ζῷον are terms 2 Peter and Jude have in common. They occur only once each elsewhere in the NT, except for the frequent use of ζῷον in Revelation.

γεγεννημένα. Prf pass ptc neut nom pl γεννάω (attributive).

φυσικὰ. Accusative of respect. In the NT, only here and in Rom 1:26.

εἰς ἅλωσιν καὶ φθορὰν. Purpose. The noun ἅλωσις ("capture," especially the taking of animals for food) is a NT *hapax legomenon*. While we have already met the rare (in the NT) word φθορά in 2 Pet 1:4, and while it has a range of meanings from "decomposition," as in the breakdown of organic matter, to "abortion" to moral "corruption" to total "destruction" (BDAG, 1054–55), here the pairing with "caught" would indicate "caught and killed" or "caught and slaughtered."

ἐν οἷς. Reference, introducing the target of βλασφημοῦντες (cf. BDAG, 13.3).

ἀγνοοῦσιν. Pres act ind 3rd pl ἀγνοέω.

βλασφημοῦντες. Pres act ptc masc nom pl βλασφημέω (attributive, "who slander," although temporal, "as they slander" or "while they slander," or causal, "because they slander," are possible).

ἐν τῇ φθορᾷ αὐτῶν καὶ φθαρήσονται. Lit. "they will also be destroyed in their destruction."

ἐν τῇ φθορᾷ. The PP is syntactically ambiguous. It could be temporal in an idiomatic cognate construction ("when they are destroyed they will also be destroyed" = "they will be utterly destroyed"), temporal with two references for the root ("when they are destroyed [physically] they will also be destroyed [eternally]"), causal with φθορᾷ meaning "corruption" ("because of their corruption they will also be destroyed"), or context/circumstance, also with φθορᾷ meaning "corruption" ("they will be destroyed in their corruption"). While φθορά normally means "corruption" in the NT (Rom 8:21; 1 Cor 15:42, 50; 2 Pet 1:4; and probably 2 Pet 2:19, with Gal 6:8 and Col 2:22 able to be read as either "corruption" or "destruction"), in this passage the use of φθορά in the first part of the verse clearly means "destruction" (and so is translated "killed"). It is more likely that φθορᾷ here alludes to the earlier use (the parallel being the reason that φθορὰν is there in the first place) than that it shifts to its other meaning without any other contextual clues. This impression is reinforced by the fact that φθείρω (see φθαρήσονται below), which is shared with Jude 10, probably refers to eternal destruction as in 1 Cor 1:17b (BDAG, 1054.3), so we also have a verb meaning "destroy" rather than "corrupt."

αὐτῶν. Objective genitive ("their destruction") or subjective genitive ("their corruption"). The antecedent could be either οὗτοι or ἄλογα ζῷα, but is probably the former assuming that ὡς ... φθορὰν is parenthetic. See further above.

φθαρήσονται. Fut pass ind 3rd pl φθείρω. The text follows 𝔓⁷² ℵ* A B C*, while ℵ²C² 𝔐 have the strengthened form καταφθαρήσονται (καταφθείρω also means "destroy," as in 2 Macc 5:14, or "ruin, corrupt," as in 2 Tim 3:8; BDAG, 529). Given the preference in the Hellenistic period for κατα- compounds and the fact that the καί right before φθαρήσονται is dropped in this reading, it looks like that καί led to hearing the familiar word.

2:13 ἀδικούμενοι μισθὸν ἀδικίας, ἡδονὴν ἡγούμενοι τὴν ἐν ἡμέρᾳ τρυφήν, σπίλοι καὶ μῶμοι ἐντρυφῶντες ἐν ταῖς ἀπάταις αὐτῶν συνευωχούμενοι ὑμῖν,

The source passage in Jude 12 reads, οὗτοί εἰσιν οἱ ἐν ταῖς ἀγάπαις ὑμῶν σπιλάδες συνευωχούμενοι ἀφόβως, and one notes the common sounds and roots (σπίλοι–σπιλάδες, ἐν ταῖς ἀπάταις –ἐν ταῖς ἀγάπαις, αὐτῶν–ὑμῶν, συνευωχούμενοι), which will influence the textual history of this verse. The series of participles in this verse and the next expand upon the reasons they will suffer destruction.

ἀδικούμενοι. Pres pass ptc masc nom pl ἀδικέω (temporal). This could be a predicate participle ("They are those who are harmed by the wages of injustice"), but a connection to the previous verse (which also uses cognates in a word play) seems to read more smoothly. This passive construction with an accusative modifier is very rare in Greek, but is probably chosen to obtain the word play. It has strong early support ($\mathfrak{P}^{72}$ ℵ* B P Ψ 1175 1243 1852 *pc*). The less objectionable κο[υ]μιούμενοι is also well attested (ℵ²A C 𝔐 *pm*). The verb κομίζω or κομέω means "to get back something that is one's own or owed to one," or, if this form were read as middle, "to receive (as recompense)" (BDAG, 557). See also Metzger, 634.

μισθὸν. Accusative of respect.

ἀδικίας. Genitive of production or means (see Wallace, 125, n. 143).

ἡδονὴν. Complement in an object-complement double accusative construction. This noun ("pleasure") is rare in the NT, appearing elsewhere only in Luke 8:14; Titus 3:3; and Jas 4:1, 3.

τὴν . . . τρυφήν. Accusative direct object of ἡγούμενοι. This noun is even rarer than ἡδονή, occurring only here and in Luke 7:25. It means "engagement in a fast, self-indulgent lifestyle" (BDAG, 1018.1). It can have a positive sense ("a state of intense satisfaction"; BDAG, 1018.3), but that is clearly not the case here. One manuscript (K) reads τροφήν ("nourishment"), raising questions about whether that scribe's monastic rule might have been so strict as to prohibit taking nourishment during the day.

ἐν ἡμέρᾳ. Temporal.

ἡγούμενοι. Pres mid ptc masc nom pl ἡγέομαι (predicate participle: "They are those who consider...").

σπίλοι καὶ μῶμοι. Predicate nominative of an implied εἰσίν. The noun σπίλος appears only here and in Eph 5:27 in the NT and means "spot, stain, blemish," either literally or figuratively (BDAG, 938). The noun μῶμος is a NT *hapax legomenon*, meaning "blame, defect, blemish" (BDAG, 663).

ἐντρυφῶντες. Pres act ptc masc nom pl ἐντρυφάω (attributive, modifying σπίλοι καὶ μῶμοι). This cognate of τρυφήν is a NT *hapax legomenon*, meaning either "to take exuberant delight in" or "to engage in self-indulgent behavior," an extension of the first meaning (BDAG, 341).

ἐν ταῖς ἀπάταις αὐτῶν. Sphere. The NA[27]/UBS[4] text is supported by 𝔓[72] ℵ A* C K 𝔐 *pm*, while A[2] B Ψ *pc* read ἐν ταῖς ἀγάπαις αὐτῶν, apparently in an attempt to conform the text to Jude 12 (see also Metzger, 634). The term ἀπάτη (seven times in the NT) means "deception, deceitfulness" or "pleasure, pleasantness," i.e., "in their desires or lusts" (BDAG, 98–99). It may be equivalent to τὰς ἐπιθυμίας τῆς ἀπάτης (Eph 4:22; "deceitful desires").

συνευωχούμενοι. Pres pass ptc masc nom pl συνευωχέομαι (temporal). This verb is used in the NT only here and in the source passage (Jude 12).

ὑμῖν. Dative complement of συνευωχούμενοι.

2:14 ὀφθαλμοὺς ἔχοντες μεστοὺς μοιχαλίδος καὶ ἀκαταπαύστους ἁμαρτίας, δελεάζοντες ψυχὰς ἀστηρίκτους, καρδίαν γεγυμνασμένην πλεονεξίας ἔχοντες, κατάρας τέκνα·

Structurally, this verse continues the list of participles found in the previous verse, adding three more (ἔχοντες, δελεάζοντες, and ἔχοντες) and closing with the nominal exclamation κατάρας τέκνα.

ὀφθαλμοὺς ... μεστοὺς ... καὶ ἀκαταπαύστους. Accusative direct object of ἔχοντες. The adjective ἀκατάπαυστος or ἀκατάπαστος (both spellings are attested) is a NT *hapax legomenon*, meaning "unceasing, restless" (BDAG, 35). It functions as a second adjectival modifier of ὀφθαλμοὺς ("they have eyes that are full of adultery and are unceasing in sin" (so BDAG, 35).

ἔχοντες. Pres act ptc masc nom pl ἔχω. This could be viewed as a predicate participle ("They are *those who have* eyes full . . .") or perhaps as an attribute participle ("who have eyes full . . ."), if one connects the adultery to the feasting.

μοιχαλίδος. Genitive of content. Lit. "eyes full of (desire for) an adultress" (BDAG, 656). This term is also used metaphorically for Israel as God's adulterous bride (Matt 12:39; Mark 8:38) and of wayward followers of Jesus (Jas 4:4). A less complex expression, ὀφθαλμοὺς ἔχοντες μεστοὺς μοιχαλίας ("having eyes full of adultery") is used in ℵ A 33 *pc*.

ἁμαρτίας. Genitive of reference or separation (BDF §182.3).

δελεάζοντες. Pres act ptc masc nom pl δελεάζω (predicate participle).

ψυχὰς ἀστηρίκτους. Accusative direct object of δελεάζοντες. The adjective ἀστήρικτος appears only in 2 Peter in the NT (also in 3:16) and means "unstable, unsteady, not settled" (Friberg, 79).

καρδίαν. Accusative direct object of ἔχοντες.

γεγυμνασμένην. Prf pass ptc fem acc sg γυμνάζω (attributive). This verb appears four times in the NT (also in Heb 5:14; 12:12; 1 Tim 4:7) in reference to exercising. MHT (3:233) believes that this verb takes a genitive complement ("exercised in/trained in greed").

ἔχοντες. Pres act ptc masc nom pl ἔχω (predicate participle).

κατάρας τέκνα. Lit. "children of cursing." MHT (4:140–43) considers the structure a Semitism (see also MHT, 2:430–501), although if it were a pure Semitism one would expect the genitive to come after the nominative it modifies. BDF (§474.4) points out that it is not a fixed rule in Greek that an anarthrous genitive must follow the anarthrous noun it modifies, giving this expression as one of the examples.

κατάρας. Attributive genitive (see also above).

τέκνα. Predicate nominative of an implied εἰσίν, the implied subject being οὗτοι (v. 12). Here, the verbless clause functions as an exclamation.

2:15 καταλείποντες εὐθεῖαν ὁδὸν ἐπλανήθησαν, ἐξακολουθήσαντες τῇ ὁδῷ τοῦ Βαλαὰμ τοῦ Βοσόρ, ὃς μισθὸν ἀδικίας ἠγάπησεν

As in the previous verse, there is a continuation of the description of οὗτοι ("these people," v. 12). Here, we have a finite verb (ἐπλανήθησαν) modified by καταλείποντες, on the one hand, and ἐξακολουθήσαντες, on the other. The following verse will expand upon Balaam, totally taking the focus off "these people," the discussion of whom will be resumed in 2:17 with another οὗτοι.

καταλείποντες. Pres act ptc masc nom pl καταλείπω (means or causal, modifying ἐπλανήθησαν; see Wallace, 630). A number of manuscripts ($\mathfrak{P}^{72}$ B² C Ψ 𝔐 *pc*) have the aorist καταλίποντες, likely viewing the action of this verb as an attendant circumstance of ἐπλανήθησαν. The NA²⁷/UBS⁴ text (ℵ A B* 33 *pc*) fits the style of 2 Peter in this passage as well as being somewhat more difficult grammatically. It is easy to see how the participle would be attracted to the tense of the finite verb or a scribe could write ι for ει, since both forms make good sense.

εὐθεῖαν ὁδὸν. Accusative direct object of καταλείποντες. In the NT, this expression elsewhere (Matt 3:3; Mark 1:3; Luke 3:5; Acts 13:10) has κυρίου between the two terms and ὁδὸν is usually first, influenced by, but not a direct quotation of, LXX Isa 40:3.

ἐπλανήθησαν. Aor pass ind 3rd pl πλανάω.

ἐξακολουθήσαντες τῇ ὁδῷ τοῦ Βαλαάμ. This idiom (lit. "following in the path of Balaam") means to imitate the behavior of Balaam (cf. BDAG, 344.2).

ἐξακολουθήσαντες. Aor act ptc masc nom pl ἐξακολουθέω (attendant circumstance, if read as modifying ἐπλανήθησαν; or a predicate participle in an elliptical construction).

τοῦ Βοσόρ. Genitive of source. There are some interesting spelling variants here. Two manuscripts (B 453) follow the normal spelling of the LXX (Βεώρ), while ℵ* combines Βεώρ and Βοσόρ (which is not found in the LXX) to form Βεωορσορ.

ὃς μισθὸν ἀδικίας ἠγάπησεν. Some important manuscripts ($\mathfrak{P}^{72}$ B) shift this to a description of "these people," i.e., the false teachers, by omitting the relative pronoun and making the verb plural, ἠγάπησαν. Codex ℵ* omits the relative pronoun but leaves the verb singular. The NA²⁷/UBS⁴ text, which follows ℵᶜ A C P Ψ 049 𝔐, fits the context, for the next verse shows that Balaam, not the false teachers, is clearly in mind.

ὅς. Nominative subject of ἠγάπησεν.
μισθὸν. Accusative direct object of ἠγάπησεν.
ἀδικίας. Attributive genitive (MHT, 3:213; BDF §165; although MHT, 2:440, calls it an objective genitive, i.e. what they love rewards their unrighteousness, this interpretation feels forced), a typical Semitism in the NT, following the LXX: "unjust reward."
ἠγάπησεν. Aor act ind 3rd sg ἀγαπάω.

2:16 ἔλεγξιν δὲ ἔσχεν ἰδίας παρανομίας· ὑποζύγιον ἄφωνον ἐν ἀνθρώπου φωνῇ φθεγξάμενον ἐκώλυσεν τὴν τοῦ προφήτου παραφρονίαν.

ἔλεγξιν. Accusative direct object of ἔσχεν. The fronting of this noun puts emphasis on his being rebuked. Lit. "he had a rebuke."
ἔσχεν. Aor act ind 3rd sg ἔχω.
ἰδίας παρανομίας. Objective genitive, "his transgression was rebuked," or genitive of reference, "He was rebuked regarding his transgression"). The noun παρανομία ("wrongdoing, evildoing, transgression," Friberg 297; or "lawnessness, evil-doing," BDAG, 769) is a NT *hapax legomenon*, but it does appear in the LXX and other Second Temple Jewish literature.
ὑποζύγιον ἄφωνον. Nominative subject of ἐκώλυσεν. The noun ὑποζύγιον appears only twice in the NT (also Matt 21:5). It can indicate any draught animal or beast of burden, but in both NT passages it refers specifically to a donkey. The adjective ἄφωνος appears four times in the NT with meanings ranging from "incapable of conveying meaning as a language normally does" (1 Cor 14:10; BDAG, 159.4) to "incapable of vocal utterance, *mute*" (1 Cor 12:2; BDAG, 159.2). Here it means "incapable of human speech, *speechless*" (BDAG, 159.3).
ἐν ... φωνῇ. Instrumental.
ἀνθρώπου. Possessive genitive. In some manuscripts ($\mathfrak{P}^{72}$ B 1241 *pc*) the dative plural ἀνθρώποις is used in place of ἀνθρώπου, presumably under the influence of ἐν (hence the dative) and to make it clearly generic (hence the plural). One scribe (Ψ) omitted φωνῇ to try to make sense of this reading, leaving ἐν ἀνθρώποις. The NA^{27}/UBS^4 text follows the majority of manuscripts.

φθεγξάμενον. Aor mid ptc neut nom sg φθέγγομαι (attendant circumstance). The verb appears three times in the NT (also v. 18 and Acts 4:18) and means to "speak, utter, proclaim... with a focus on the act of utterance" (BDAG, 1054).

ἐκώλυσεν. Aor act ind 3rd sg κωλύω.

τὴν... παραφρονίαν. Accusative direct object of ἐκώλυσεν. The noun παραφρονία—an example of an abstract substantive built from an adjective (BDF §110.2)—is a NT *hapax legomenon* meaning "state or condition of irrationality, madness, insanity" (BDAG, 772). While prophets were sometimes thought to be somewhat "off" by their fellow-citizens, the contrast between a prophet (who should hear from God but is caught in evil-doing by a donkey) and a donkey (which speaks, presumably from God, to stop the prophet's insanity or irrationality) would not have been lost on the readers.

τοῦ προφήτου. Subjective genitive.

2:17 Οὗτοί εἰσιν πηγαὶ ἄνυδροι καὶ ὁμίχλαι ὑπὸ λαίλαπος ἐλαυνόμεναι, οἷς ὁ ζόφος τοῦ σκότους τετήρηται.

Οὗτοί. Nominative subject of εἰσιν. The author uses the demonstrative pronoun to signal a shift from Balaam back to the false teachers he has been denouncing, moving his topic from greed to licentiousness.

εἰσιν. Pres act ind 3rd pl εἰμί.

πηγαὶ ἄνυδροι καὶ ὁμίχλαι. Predicate nominative. Jude 12 has νεφέλαι ἄνυδροι ὑπὸ ἀνέμων παραφερόμεναι, which draws a contrast between promise, in being clouds, and disappointment, in that they are waterless. Second Peter has a starker contrast between πηγή ("spring, fountain") and ἄνυδρος ("without water, waterless"), which is paradoxical in that the concept of "spring" implies something with water.

ὁμίχλαι ὑπὸ λαίλαπος ἐλαυνόμεναι. While the grammar is clear enough, the terms themselves are unusual. Whereas Jude 12 has νεφέλη, 2 Peter uses ὁμίχλη, a NT *hapax legomenon* meaning "an atmospheric condition that darkens the sky... mist, fog" (BDAG, 705). This is changed in 𝔐 to the more familiar νεφέλαι, which conforms to Jude 12. Whereas Jude 12 has the normal term for wind, ἄνεμος, 2 Peter uses λαῖλαψ ("whirlwind, hurricane"; BDAG, 581), found in the NT only here and in Mark 4:37 and Luke 8:23. Therefore, 2 Peter must also use a strong verb, ἐλαύνω ("to urge or propel along, drive"; BDAG, 314), which appears only five times in the NT, rather than Jude's milder παραφερόμεναι ("carried along/about" or "borne along").

ὑπὸ λαίλαπος. Ultimate agency.

ἐλαυνόμεναι. Pres pass ptc fem nom pl ἐλαύνω (attributive).

οἷς. Dative of disadvantage.

ὁ ζόφος. Nominative subject of τετήρηται. While ζόφος has already appeared in 2 Pet 2:4 (following Jude 6), the somewhat pleonastic combination here with τοῦ σκότους comes directly from Jude 13. The NA²⁷/UBS⁴ text is supported by 𝔓⁷² ℵ B Ψ *pc*, while many manuscripts (A C L P 33 *pm*) conform the text to Jude 13 by adding εἰς αἰῶνα.

τοῦ σκότους. Attributive ("dark gloom") or epexegetical genitive ("the gloom, that is, the darkness"; so BDAG 932.1; cf. BDF §167). The identical expression occurs in Jude 13.

τετήρηται. Prf pass ind 3rd sg τηρέω.

2:18 ὑπέρογκα γὰρ ματαιότητος φθεγγόμενοι δελεάζουσιν ἐν ἐπιθυμίαις σαρκὸς ἀσελγείαις τοὺς ὀλίγως ἀποφεύγοντας τοὺς ἐν πλάνῃ ἀναστρεφομένους,

ὑπέρογκα . . . ματαιότητος φθεγγόμενοι. Lit. "uttering boastful (words) of nonsense."

ὑπέρογκα. Accusative direct object of φθεγγόμενοι. Found in the NT only here and in Jude 16, the adjective ὑπέρογκος means "of excessive size, overgrown," and thus in this context, "boastful, bombastic, pompous" (Friberg, 390).

γάρ. Causal.

ματαιότητος. Found three times in the NT (also Rom 8:20; Eph 4:17), the noun ματαιότης means "nonsense, nothingness, emptiness" (Friberg, 254).

φθεγγόμενοι. Pres mid ptc masc nom pl φθέγγομαι (means). The verb is found in the NT only here, verse 16, and in Acts 4:18. It means to "speak, utter, proclaim . . . with a focus on the act of utterance" (BDAG, 1054).

δελεάζουσιν. Pres act ind 3rd pl δελεάζω. This rare verb (for the NT) was also used in verse 14.

ἐν ἐπιθυμίαις. Instrumental.

σαρκὸς. Attributive or subjective genitive.

ἀσελγείαις. Dative of instrument, in apposition to ἐν ἐπιθυμίαις.

τοὺς ... ἀποφεύγοντας. Pres act ptc masc acc pl ἀποφεύγω (substantival). Accusative direct object of δελεάζουσιν. This verb appears in the NT only in 2 Peter (also v. 20 and 1:4). The 𝔐 tradition substitutes an aorist participle here (ἀποφύγοντας; as in v. 20), which fits better with the reading ὄντως (see below on ὀλίγως) since the aorist participle could imply that the escape was completed rather than in progress as the present participle implies.

ὀλίγως. This adverb is a relatively new word in Greek (MHT, 2:163; BDF §102.6) and a NT *hapax legomenon* meaning "scarcely, barely" (BDAG, 703). It appears in 𝔓⁷² ℵ A B Ψ 33 *pc*. Many manuscripts (ℵ* C P 𝔐), however, use the older Greek word ὄντως ("really, certainly, in truth"; BDAG, 715), which occurs 10 times in the NT. Both the manuscript evidence and the fact that it is the less common word (harder reading) favor the reading ὀλίγως.

τοὺς ... ἀναστρεφομένους. Pres pass ptc masc acc pl ἀναστρέφω (substantival). Accusative direct object of ἀποφεύγοντας. In the passive (or perhaps middle) voice, this verb has an active sense, either "to spend time in a locality, *stay, live*" or "to conduct oneself in terms of certain principles, *act, behave, conduct oneself, live*" (BDAG, 72.3.b). The type of behavior is described by ἐν πλάνῃ here.

ἐν πλάνῃ. Manner.

2:19 ἐλευθερίαν αὐτοῖς ἐπαγγελλόμενοι, αὐτοὶ δοῦλοι ὑπάρχοντες τῆς φθορᾶς· ᾧ γάρ τις ἥττηται, τούτῳ δεδούλωται.

The focus shifts from the victims back to the the false teachers in this verse. While the grammar looks similar to the beginning of verse 18, in reality we appear to have a participle functioning as a nominative absolute modified by a concessive adverbial participle and followed by a short complex sentence that is like a pithy proverb serving as a parenthetical remark that supports the nominative absolute.

ἐλευθερίαν. Accusative direct object of ἐπαγγελλόμενοι.

αὐτοῖς. Dative indirect object of ἐπαγγελλόμενοι.

ἐπαγγελλόμενοι. Pres mid ptc masc nom pl ἐπαγγέλλομαι (attendant circumstance).

αὐτοί. Nominative intensive subject of ὑπάρχοντες.

δοῦλοι. Predicate nominative.

ὑπάρχοντες. Pres act ptc masc nom pl ὑπάρχω (concessive). The fact that ὑπάρχω is "a widely used substitute in Hellenistic Greek for εἶναι" (BDAG, 1029.2) likely led A and a few other manuscripts to substitute ὄντες.

τῆς φθορᾶς. Possessive ("they are slaves of corruption," their metaphorical master), or objective genitive ("they serve corruption").

ᾧ γάρ τις ἥττηται, τούτῳ δεδούλωται. This sentence is parenthetical.

ᾧ. Dative complement of ἥττηται if the verb is middle ("succumb to") or dative of instrument (MHT, 3:240; cf. BDF §191.4; see also v. 20) if the verb is passive ("be conquered by").

γάρ. Causal. Either because the saying was often stated this way (if it were truly proverbial) or to add more force, some manuscripts (ℵ A C P Ψ 048 𝔐) add an adverbial καί ("also" or "even") between τούτῳ and δεδούλωται. The more concise NA[27]/UBS[4] text has strong early support ($\mathfrak{P}$[72] ℵ* B *pc*).

ἥττηται. Prf mid ind 3rd sg ἡττάομαι. This verb is used only three times in the NT (also v. 20 and 2 Cor 12:13). It only appears in the middle (although traditionally it has been considered passive) in the New Testament, Second Temple, and early Christian literature. Here, the meaning is "to be vanquished, be defeated, succumb" (BDAG, 441.1). The use of ττ where one might expect σσ is rare in Hellenisitic Greek, but does appear in words that are especially Attic and in texts influenced by the Atticistic movement (so BDF §34.1).

δεδούλωται. Prf pass ind 3rd sg δουλόω. On the voice, see MHT, 3:56.

2:20 εἰ γὰρ ἀποφυγόντες τὰ μιάσματα τοῦ κόσμου ἐν ἐπιγνώσει τοῦ κυρίου [ἡμῶν] καὶ σωτῆρος Ἰησοῦ Χριστοῦ, τούτοις δὲ πάλιν ἐμπλακέντες ἡττῶνται, γέγονεν αὐτοῖς τὰ ἔσχατα χείρονα τῶν πρώτων.

The subject of this verse (reinforced by the theological statement of the next verse and then the proverb of verse 22) is most likely the false teachers (fitting with the whole series of nominative masculine plural participles and pronouns), although it could also apply to those whom they have deceived by false promises of freedom.

εἰ. Introduces a first class condition.

γὰρ. Explanatory.

ἀποφυγόντες. Aor act ptc masc nom pl ἀποφεύγω (temporal).

τὰ μιάσματα. Accusative direct object of ἀποφυγόντες (see also BDF §149). The noun μίασμα is a NT *hapax legomenon* referring to the "defilement connected with a crime" and so meaning "shameful deed, misdeed, crime," where the focus is on the crime itself (BDAG, 650).

τοῦ κόσμου. Genitive of source or possessive genitive.

ἐν ἐπιγνώσει. Instrumental.

τοῦ κυρίου . . . καὶ σωτῆρος. Objective genitive. The idea here is already found in 1:2-3. The single article indicates that one individual is being described (see 1:1 on τοῦ θεοῦ ἡμῶν καὶ σωτῆρος Ἰησοῦ Χριστοῦ).

[ἡμῶν]. Genitive of subordination. Both Codex B and 𝔐 omit ἡμῶν, which tends to make the role of Jesus the Anointed One more absolute. The NA²⁷/UBS⁴ text has strong support (𝔓⁷² ℵ A C P Ψ *pm*).

Ἰησοῦ Χριστοῦ. Genitive in apposition to τοῦ κυρίου . . . καὶ σωτῆρος. See also Jude 1 on Χριστοῦ.

τούτοις. Dative complement of ἡττῶνται or dative of agency, if ἡττῶνται is read as passive (cf. BDF §191.4; see also v. 19).

ἐμπλακέντες. Aor pass ptc masc nom pl ἐμπλέκω (causal).

ἡττῶνται. Pres mid ind 3rd pl ἡττάομαι. See also verse 19 on ἥττηται. MHT (3:62) calls this a perfective present, but it would be semantically more accurate to simply say that as a present tense this verb has imperfective aspect, "*the action is conceived of by the language user as being in progress*" (Porter, 21, italics in original).

γέγονεν αὐτοῖς τὰ ἔσχατα χείρονα τῶν πρώτων. The apodosis of the conditional sentence.

γέγονεν. Prf act ind 3rd sg γίνομαι. Here, the verb points to a change in nature or state (see BDAG, 198.5).

αὐτοῖς. Dative of respect.

τὰ ἔσχατα. Nominative subject of γέγονεν.
χείρονα. Predicate adjective. This functions as the comparative form of κακός.
τῶν πρώτων. Genitive of comparison.

2:21 κρεῖττον γὰρ ἦν αὐτοῖς μὴ ἐπεγνωκέναι τὴν ὁδὸν τῆς δικαιοσύνης ἢ ἐπιγνοῦσιν ὑποστρέψαι ἐκ τῆς παραδοθείσης αὐτοῖς ἁγίας ἐντολῆς.

κρεῖττον. Predicate adjective.
γὰρ. Causal.
ἦν. Impf act ind 3rd sg εἰμί. The imperfect is being used in a contrary to fact situation, although this is not formally a conditional sentence (so BDF §358.1; MHT, 3:90, demures, arguing that "a present obligation is expressed for some reason in the imperfect").
αὐτοῖς. Dative of advantage or reference. BDF (§410) claims that the use of a dative as an adjunct to the subject of an infinitive is relatively rare," but it is more likely that the pronoun is part of the main clause than the infinitival clause here.
ἐπεγνωκέναι. Prf act inf ἐπιγινώσκω. The infinitival clause, μὴ ἐπεγνωκέναι τὴν ὁδὸν τῆς δικαιοσύνης, functions as the subject of ἦν. Lit. "Not to have known the way of righteousness would have been better for them."
τὴν ὁδὸν. Accusative direct object of ἐπεγνωκέναι. MHT (3:149) points to this passage as an example of where the infinitive + accusative structure is "classically correct."
τῆς δικαιοσύνης. Attributive genitive; here, a Hebraism (MHT, 4:142).
ἐπιγνοῦσιν. Aor act pct masc dat pl ἐπιγινώσκω (temporal, "after they knew it," or substantival, dative of disadvantage). The participle is parallel to αὐτοῖς in this elliptical construction: "Not to have known the way of righteousness would have been better *for them* than to turn from the holy command that had been passed on to them would be *for those who knew [it]*."
ὑποστρέψαι. Aor act inf ὑποστρέφω. The infinitival clause, ὑποστρέψαι ἐκ τῆς παραδοθείσης αὐτοῖς ἁγίας ἐντολῆς, functions as the subject of an implied form of εἰμί. The 𝔐 tradition reads ἐπιστρέψαι (in what seems to be a case of dittography given the

prefix of the preceding participle), while ℵ A Ψ *pc* have the more expansive εἰς τὰ ὀπίσω ἀνακάμψει ἀπό in place of ὑποστρέψαι ἐκ.

ἐκ ... ἁγίας ἐντολῆς. Separation.

παραδοθείσης. Aor pass ptc fem gen sg παραδίδωμι (attributive).

αὐτοῖς. Dative indirect object of παραδοθείσης.

2:22 συμβέβηκεν αὐτοῖς τὸ τῆς ἀληθοῦς παροιμίας· Κύων ἐπιστρέψας ἐπὶ τὸ ἴδιον ἐξέραμα, καί, Ὗς λουσαμένη εἰς κυλισμὸν βορβόρου.

συμβέβηκεν αὐτοῖς τὸ τῆς ἀληθοῦς παροιμίας. On the proverbial form, see MHT, 1:238, 156.

συμβέβηκεν. Prf act ind 3rd sg συμβαίνω. This verb occurs eight times in the NT and means either "to join someone in going somewhere, go along with" or, as here, "to occur as event or process, happen, come about" (BDAG, 956).

τὸ ... παροιμίας. Nominative subject of συμβέβηκεν. Lit. "The true proverb has happened to them." The term παροιμία ("proverb, proverbial saying"; Friberg, 301) occurs only five times in the NT, here and four times in John.

τῆς ἀληθοῦς. Attributive genitive.

Κύων ἐπιστρέψας ἐπὶ τὸ ἴδιον ἐξέραμα. As is not surprising in a proverb, the vocabulary is relatively rare. Dogs were not viewed as useful animals in the Jewish world, but rather were considered unclean. The term κύων occurs five times in the NT, often with negative connotations (Phil 3:2; Rev 22:15); so a negative tone is probably implied here. On the diminutive morphology, see BDF §111.3. The word for "vomit" ἐξέραμα is a NT *hapax legomenon*.

Κύων. Nominative absolute. Proverbs are in essence a formulaic ellipsis (BDF §480.5; see also Wallace, 54–55).

ἐπιστρέψας. Aor act ptc masc nom sg ἐπιστρέφω (attributive).

ἐπὶ τὸ ἴδιον ἐξέραμα. Locative.

Ὗς λουσαμένη εἰς κυλισμὸν βορβόρου. Again, the proverbial saying is full of rare words with Ὗς ("sow") being a NT *hapax legomenon* (and in the process of being replaced by χοῖρος: BDF §126.1.a.α), while λούω ("to wash") occurs only five times. The terms κυλισμός ("rolling, wallowing"; BDAG, 574) and βόρβορος ("slime, mud, mire," Friberg 93; a classical word found only in

LXX Jer 46:6 elsewhere in biblical Greek; see MHT, 2:363) are also *hapax legomena*. Some manuscripts (ℵ A C² Ψ 𝔐 *pc*) read κύλισμα, probably due to the previous ἐξέραμα, although the term does occur in Symmachus' translation of Ezek 10:13. The text is found in 𝔓⁷² B C* *pc*.

Ὗς. Nominative absolute (see also above on Κύων).

λουσαμένη. Aor mid ptc fem nom sg λούω (attributive). MHT (1:156–57) cites this as an example showing that the middle voice is not in essence reflexive.

εἰς κυλισμὸν. Locative, with a form of ἐπιστρέφω implied.

Βορβόρου. Attributive genitive: lit. "muddy rolling."

2 Peter 3:1-7

¹This is now the second letter that I have written to you, loved ones, in which I, by way of remembrance, stir up your sincere way of thinking ²to remember the words that were previously spoken by the holy prophets and the command of your official delegates, (sent by) the Lord and Savior. ³Know this first of all, that in the last days mockers will come with mockery, living in accordance with their own desires ⁴and saying, "Where is the promise of his coming? For, since (our) ancestors passed away, everything remains just as (it was) from the beginning of creation." ⁵For they consciously avoid noticing this: that the heavens existed long ago and the earth has come to exist by God's word from and through water, ⁶through which the world at that time was destroyed, being inundated by water. ⁷And the present heavens and earth have been reserved for fire by this same word and are being kept for the day of judgment and destruction of impious people.

The change of subject (seen in the reference to the letter, Ταύτην ἤδη ... δευτέραν ... ἐπιστολήν) and the vocative ἀγαπητοί indicate the transition to a new paragraph, which discusses another aspect of the false teachers, namely, their denial of divine judgment.

3:1 Ταύτην ἤδη, ἀγαπητοί, δευτέραν ὑμῖν γράφω ἐπιστολήν, ἐν αἷς διεγείρω ὑμῶν ἐν ὑπομνήσει τὴν εἰλικρινῆ διάνοιαν.

Ταύτην ἤδη ... δευτέραν ὑμῖν γράφω ἐπιστολήν. Lit. "I am writing this second letter to you now." Although it is unremarkable to have the direct object in the clause final position, the fact that its two modifiers (Ταύτην and δευτέραν) are separated from it *and* placed in two other positions in the clause is unusual, although found in classical Greek (MHT, 3:192).

Ταύτην ... δευτέραν ... ἐπιστολήν. Accusative direct object of γράφω.

ἀγαπητοί. Vocative.

ὑμῖν. Dative indirect object of γράφω.

γράφω. Pres act ind 1st sg γράφω.

ἐν αἷς. Locative. A *constructio ad sensum*, i.e., grammatically the relative pronoun should be a feminine dative singular agreeing with ἐπιστολήν, but since it is the second letter and both letters are in view, the plural is used (BDF §296).

διεγείρω. Pres act ind 1st sg διεγείρω.

ὑμῶν. Possessive genitive, modifying τὴν εἰλικρινῆ διάνοιαν.

ἐν ὑπομνήσει. Instrumental. See also 1:13 on the same verb and PP.

τὴν εἰλικρινῆ διάνοιαν. Accusative direct object of διεγείρω. The adjective εἰλικρινής ("sincere," "pure") occurs only twice in the NT (also Phil 1:10).

3:2 μνησθῆναι τῶν προειρημένων ῥημάτων ὑπὸ τῶν ἁγίων προφητῶν καὶ τῆς τῶν ἀποστόλων ὑμῶν ἐντολῆς τοῦ κυρίου καὶ σωτῆρος,

μνησθῆναι. Aor pass inf μιμνήσκω (purpose).

τῶν ... ῥημάτων ... καὶ τῆς ... ἐντολῆς. Genitive direct object of μνησθῆναι (see also Jude 17 on τῶν ῥημάτων).

προειρημένων. Prf pass ptc neut gen pl προεῖπον (attributive). On the separation of the participle from its adjuncts, see BDF §474.5.a.

ὑπὸ τῶν ἁγίων προφητῶν. Ultimate agency. Jude 19, which 2 Peter alludes to but does not quote, identifies Enoch as one of these.

τῆς τῶν ἀποστόλων ὑμῶν ἐντολῆς τοῦ κυρίου καὶ σωτῆρος. There is a long string of genitives with different functions here.

τῆς ... ἐντολῆς. Part of the genitive direct object of μνησθῆναι (see above).

τῶν ἀποστόλων. Subjective genitive.

ὑμῶν. Genitive of relationship, indicating to whom the apostles/delegates were sent.

τοῦ κυρίου καὶ σωτῆρος. It is clear from the Granville-Sharp Rule that τοῦ κυρίου καὶ σωτῆρος refers to a single individual (Wallace, 274). More difficult is determining the relationship of the genitives to ἐντολῆς, which in contrast to τῶν ... ῥημάτων is singular and thus refers either to the teaching of Jesus as a whole or the basic command of the good news to commit to Jesus as Lord. The phrase may be taken as a subjective genitive, modifying τῶν ἀποστόλων (see also 1:1). MHT (3:218), however, suggests that *perhaps* both τῶν ἀποστόλων and τοῦ κυρίου καὶ σωτῆρος modify the same noun: "the commandment of the Lord and Savior transmitted by the apostles to you" (see also BDF §168.1).

3:3 τοῦτο πρῶτον γινώσκοντες ὅτι ἐλεύσονται ἐπ' ἐσχάτων τῶν ἡμερῶν [ἐν] ἐμπαιγμονῇ ἐμπαῖκται κατὰ τὰς ἰδίας ἐπιθυμίας αὐτῶν πορευόμενοι

τοῦτο. Accusative direct object of γινώσκοντες. The demonstrative pronoun points forward to the ὅτι clause.

πρῶτον. This form could be an adverb of degree: "in the first place, above all, especially" (BDAG, 894.2.b). Or, less likely, it could be an accusative adjective that serves as the complement in an object-complement double accusative construction: "knowing this (to be) foremost" (NET Bible).

γινώσκοντες. Pres act ptc masc nom pl γινώσκω. Imperatival, which is well known in Peter and Paul (MHT, 3:343; BDF §468.2). MHT (3:343) further clarifies that an implied imperative ἐστέ should be "understood as a copula with all these ptcs., which therefore do not constitute an anacolouthon."

ὅτι. Introduces a clause that is epexegetical to τοῦτο.

ἐλεύσονται. Fut mid ind 3rd pl ἔρχομαι.

ἐπ' ἐσχάτων τῶν ἡμερῶν. Temporal. The ἐσχάτων is an anarthrous substantival adjective (BDF §264.5). While some later manuscripts (e.g., 𝔐) have the singular ἐσχάτου, all earlier manuscripts have the plural form, either by attraction to the plural ἡμερῶν or because they think of τὰ ἔσχατα (as in *Barn.* 16.5 and Hermas, *Sim.* 9.12.13). This use of ἐσχάτων with the genitive τῶν ἡμερῶν is Semitic (BDF §234.8).

[ἐν] ἐμπαιγμονῇ ἐμπαῖκται. Instrumental (ἐν) or dative of instrument. The NA²⁷/UBS⁴ text follows ℵ A B Ψ *pc*. Some manuscripts omit the ἐν (𝔓⁷² C P *pc*), while 𝔐 omits both ἐν and ἐμπαιγμονῇ. The text is a tautology, one of various forms of Semitisms in the NT (MHT, 2:420; cf. MHT, 4:143). The noun ἐμπαιγμονή ("mocking, ridicule, derision"; Friberg, 146) is a NT *hapax legomenon*, while ἐμπαίκτης ("one who makes fun of another, mocker, scoffer"; Friberg, 146) is found only here and in the parallel in Jude 18.

κατὰ τὰς ἰδίας ἐπιθυμίας αὐτῶν. Standard. The use of ἴδιος conforms to classical usage, i.e., ἴδιος as opposed to κοινός, "their own" as opposed to the "common" or "shared." The combination of ἴδιος with αὐτῶν is common in both classical and Modern Greek usage and is not emphatic (BDF §285.1; MHT, 3:191–92), having two words that both mean "their" was pleonastic enough that ℵ and A reverse ἐπιθυμίας and αὐτῶν, and 𝔓⁷² omits αὐτῶν.

πορευόμενοι. Pres mid ptc masc pl nom πορεύομαι (attributive or manner).

3:4 καὶ λέγοντες· Ποῦ ἐστιν ἡ ἐπαγγελία τῆς παρουσίας αὐτοῦ; ἀφ' ἧς γὰρ οἱ πατέρες ἐκοιμήθησαν, πάντα οὕτως διαμένει ἀπ' ἀρχῆς κτίσεως.

The verse consists of the participle (linked by καί to πορευόμενοι in the previous verse) introducing a two-clause quotation.

λέγοντες. Pres act ptc masc nom pl λέγω (attributive or manner). Introduces direct discourse.

Ποῦ. Predicate interrogative adverb.

ἐστιν. Pres act ind 3rd sg εἰμί.

ἡ ἐπαγγελία. Nominative subject of ἐστιν.

τῆς παρουσίας. Objective genitive.

αὐτοῦ. Subjective genitive.

ἀφ' ἧς. This phrase may involve the ellipsis of ἡμέρα (so BDF §240.2), but as MHT (3:17) states, "the phrase is virtually a conjunction." Similarly, Wallace (343) views this as an "adverbial conjunctive use."

γὰρ. Causal.

οἱ πατέρες. Nominative subject of ἐκοιμήθησαν.

ἐκοιμήθησαν. Aor mid ind 3rd pl κοιμάομαι. On the voice, see "Deponency" in the Series Introduction.

πάντα. Nominative subject of διαμένει.

οὕτως. Adverb of manner.

διαμένει. Pres act ind 3rd sg διαμένω. This verb appears only five times in the NT (also Luke 1:22; 22:8; Gal 2:5; Heb 1:11). Although MHT (3:62) states that the present tense indicates "the continuance of an action during the past and up to the moment of speaking," that nuance seems to stem from the verb διαμένω rather than the tense.

ἀπ' ἀρχῆς. Temporal. References to creation of the world are regularly anarthrous in the expression ἀπ' ἀρχῆς (BDF §235.4).

κτίσεως. Subjective genitive.

3:5 λανθάνει γὰρ αὐτοὺς τοῦτο θέλοντας ὅτι οὐρανοὶ ἦσαν ἔκπαλαι καὶ γῆ ἐξ ὕδατος καὶ δι' ὕδατος συνεστῶσα τῷ τοῦ θεοῦ λόγῳ,

λανθάνει. Pres act ind 3rd sg λανθάνω. The verb λανθάνω occurs only six times in the NT, twice in this chapter. Its basic meaning is "to succeed in avoiding attention or awareness, *escape notice, be hidden*," and so it often occurs, as here, in an impersonal expression with an accusative "λανθάνει τί τινα *something is hidden from someone, escapes someone's notice*" (BDAG 586). Thus in this verse "this" (τοῦτο) is hidden from "them" (αὐτοὺς; BDF §149; see also v. 8).

γὰρ. Explanatory.

αὐτοὺς. Accusative of respect. In the construction with λανθάνει (see above), this accusative element refers to the one from whom something is hidden ("This escapes *their* notice"; see also v. 8 on ὑμᾶς).

τοῦτο. In the construction with λανθάνει (see above), the demonstrative pronoun could be viewed as its nominative subject (thus the singular verb; lit. "this escapes notice") or perhaps the accusative direct object of λανθάνει.

θέλοντας. Pres act ptc masc acc pl θέλω (manner). The accusative case reflects the fact that αὐτοὺς is the conceptual ("they willfully ignore") but not grammatical subject of λανθάνει.

ὅτι. Introduces a clause that is epexegetical to τοῦτο. The ὅτι clause continues into the next verse.

οὐρανοί. Nominative subject of ἦσαν. This noun is typically anarthrous, as here (MHT, 3:174–75).

ἦσαν. Impf act ind 3rd pl εἰμί.

ἔκπαλαι. This adverb (pertaining to "a point of time long before the current moment, long ago"; BDAG, 307) is found only here and in 2:3 in the NT. It is a compound adverb formed with a prepositional prefix (ἐκ-), characteristic of "the later [Greek] language" (BDF §116.3).

καί. The conjunction seems to introduce a new clause rather than linking γῆ to οὐρανοί, given the number and gender of συνεστῶσα, although see below on γῆ.

γῆ. Nominative subject of (ἦσαν) συνεστῶσα. This is not typically anarthrous, except in combination with οὐρανός (MHT, 3:174–75), so its anarthrous state raises the possibility that the καί does link it with οὐρανοί and that συνεστῶσα, perhaps because of its distance from οὐρανοί has been attracted to γῆ in number and gender.

ἐξ ὕδατος καὶ δι' ὕδατος. While Wallace (432, 435) argues that this is an example of "impersonal means" (after ἐκ) and "intermediate agency" (after διά) with a passive verb, with λόγῳ below being a dative of (impersonal) means, it is simpler to view ἐξ ὕδατος as source and δι' ὕδατος as means.

συνεστῶσα. Prf act ptc fem nom sg συνίστημι. There are two possible explanations of the grammar here. (1) Since the participle agrees with γῆ in number and gender, it is best not to view ἦσαν ... συνεστῶσα as a periphrastic construction having οὐρανοὶ ... καὶ γῆ as its subject (for which we would expect a masculine plural participle). Instead, οὐρανοὶ alone serves as the subject of ἦσαν, with γῆ serving as the subject of an *implied* pluperfect periphrastic construction with ἦσαν being left out by ellipsis (cf. MHT, 3:89).

In the active voice with γῆ as the subject, the verb must mean, "to come to be in a condition of coherence, *continue, endure, exist, hold together*" (BDAG, 973.B.3). See the translation above, which follows the NRSV, NASV, and most other contemporary translations. (2) Since οὐρανοὶ καὶ γῆ are an established pair (see v. 7 below), one does have a periphrastic construction with οὐρανοὶ ... καὶ γῆ as the subject and ἦσαν ... συνεστῶσα as the verb, with συνεστῶσα having been attracted in gender and number to γῆ, which is closest to it and separated from οὐρανοὶ ἦσαν. The verb, being in a periphrastic passive construction, therefore means "to bring into existence in an organized manner, *put together, constitute, establish, prepare*" (BDAG, 973.A.4). The passage could then be translated: "the heavens and earth came into existence long ago by God's word from and through water." There is a textual issue that arose due to the fact that the –μι forms of the perfect of this verb are in retreat in the Hellenstic period—Friberg (368) lists the lemma as "συνίστημι and συνιστάνω (and συνιστάω)"—so the form of the participle varies among the manuscripts as does their understanding of the grammar. The NA^{27}/UBS^4 text is supported by ℵ^c A C P 𝔐 *pc*; while ℵ* Ψ *pc* have συνεστῶτα, 𝔓^{72} and B read συνεστῶση, and K has συνεστῶσαι.

τῷ ... λόγῳ. Dative of instrument (Wallace, 163).

τοῦ θεοῦ. Genitive of source or subjective genitive.

3:6 δι' ὧν ὁ τότε κόσμος ὕδατι κατακλυσθεὶς ἀπώλετο·

This relative clause closes the sentence that began in verse 5.

δι' ὧν. Intermediate agency. The plural form eliminates τῷ τοῦ θεοῦ λόγῳ as the single antecedent. The plural ὧν is either due to the double reference to ὕδατος (ἐξ ὕδατος καὶ δι' ὕδατος), and so reflects a *constructio ad sensum*, or it could have both τῷ τοῦ θεοῦ λόγῳ and δι' ὕδατος as its antecedent.

τότε. Attributive use of a correlative adverb of time, clearly marked by the adverb's attributive position between article and noun (MHT, 3:222; BDAG, 1012). This classical construction is rare in the NT and it is always used for time: "the then world" or "the then-existing world."

ὕδατι. Dative of instrument.

κατακλυσθείς. Aor pass ptc masc nom sg κατακλύζω (means). Wallace (629) notes that means participles usually follow the verb, but here the participle precedes the verb, thus allowing the clause to end with "perished." The verb itself is a NT *hapax legomenon*, although it is found in the LXX (MHT, 4:143).

ἀπώλετο. Aor mid ind 3rd sg ἀπόλλυμι.

3:7 οἱ δὲ νῦν οὐρανοὶ καὶ ἡ γῆ τῷ αὐτῷ λόγῳ τεθησαυρισμένοι εἰσὶν πυρὶ τηρούμενοι εἰς ἡμέραν κρίσεως καὶ ἀπωλείας τῶν ἀσεβῶν ἀνθρώπων.

In contrast to what happen to ὁ τότε κόσμος, this verse describes the present situation of οἱ οὐρανοὶ καὶ ἡ γῆ. This rounds out the paragraph, for the next paragraph is about what the readers are not to forget in contrast to what the false teachers have forgotten.

οἱ ... νῦν οὐρανοὶ καὶ ἡ γῆ. Nominative subject of τεθησαυρισμένοι εἰσίν.

νῦν. Attributive use of a correlative adverb of time (see also v. 6 on τότε).

τῷ αὐτῷ λόγῳ. Dative of instrument. There is some textual divergence over the use of αὐτός. In the NA²⁷/UBS⁴ text (which follows 𝔓⁷² A B P Ψ 33 *al*) it is the dative intensive pronoun αὐτῷ ("by the same word"). Some manuscripts (ℵ C 𝔐), however, have the (subjective) genitive αὐτοῦ: "by his word." This is a secondary reading that clarifies the parallel to τοῦ θεοῦ in verse 5.

τεθησαυρισμένοι. Prf pass ptc masc nom pl θησαυρίζω (perfect periphrastic; cf. MHT, 3:89).

εἰσὶν. Pres act ind 3rd pl εἰμί.

πυρί. Dative of purpose ("for fire"), functioning the same as εἰς below, although some manuscripts (C* P *al*) read ἐν πυρί (locative); or perhaps, instrumental, making the function parallel to ὕδατι in verse 6.

τηρούμενοι. Pres pass ptc masc nom pl τηρέω (attendant circumstance, although MHT (3:88) views it as present periphrastic). If MHT is correct, the sense would be "the present heaven and earth, which have been stored up by this same word, are being kept for fire on the day of judgment." The lack of a καί, however, raises questions about the validity of this reading.

εἰς ἡμέραν κρίσεως καὶ ἀπωλείας. Purpose/goal.

τῶν ἀσεβῶν ἀνθρώπων. Objective genitive. The plural may form an *inclusio* in terms of number and subject matter with ἐμπαῖκται in 3:3, the shift from the fate of the world to the fate of impious people closing off the paragraph.

2 Peter 3:8-9

⁸And don't you forget this one thing, loved ones: One day is as a thousand years before the Lord and a thousand years as one day. ⁹The Lord is not slow about his promises, as some think of slowness, but he is patient toward you, not wishing anyone to be destroyed, but all to arrive at repentance.

The vocative ἀγαπητοί and the address to "you" signal a new paragraph, which is tied into the previous paragraph by the repetition of vocabulary: λανθανέτω and ἐπαγγελίας, not to mention the cognates ἀπωλείας/ἀπολέσθαι, all used to contrast "you" or "the Lord" with the situation of the "mockers."

3:8 Ἓν δὲ τοῦτο μὴ λανθανέτω ὑμᾶς, ἀγαπητοί, ὅτι μία ἡμέρα παρὰ κυρίῳ ὡς χίλια ἔτη καὶ χίλια ἔτη ὡς ἡμέρα μία.

Whereas the previous paragraph had "them" forgetting, this paragraph begins with the "loved ones" being admonished not to forget. What they are not to forget is expressed in a compound nominal sentence.

Ἓν ... τοῦτο. Nominative subject of λανθανέτω (see also v. 5). 𝔓⁷² *al* read ἐν δὲ τούτῳ ("and in this"), probably because Ἓν and ἐν and τοῦτο and τούτῳ sounded the same and so the more common construction was heard.

λανθανέτω. Pres act impv 3rd sg λανθάνω (prohibition). See also verse 5 on λανθάνει.

ὑμᾶς. Accusative of respect. This is a use of the accusative with a verb of fearing, fleeing, avoiding, forgetting, swearing, etc. (BDF §149; see also v. 5 on αὐτοὺς).

ἀγαπητοί. Vocative, functioning as a virtual appositive to ὑμᾶς.
ὅτι. Introduces a clause that is epexegetical to Ἐν . . . τοῦτο.
μία ἡμέρα. Nominative subject in a verbless equative clause.
παρὰ κυρίῳ. Here, παρά with the dative is "a marker of whose viewpoint is relevant, *in the sight or judgment of someone*" (BDAG, 757.2).
ὡς χίλια . . . ὡς ἡμέρα μία. Here, ὡς is used as an adjective in the predicate position, perhaps due to Semitic influence (BDAG, 1104.2.c.β).
καὶ χίλια ἔτη. Perhaps due to haplography, this phrase is missing in both 𝔓⁷² and ℵ.
χίλια ἔτη. Nominative subject in a verbless equative clause.

3:9 οὐ βραδύνει κύριος τῆς ἐπαγγελίας, ὥς τινες βραδύτητα ἡγοῦνται, ἀλλὰ μακροθυμεῖ εἰς ὑμᾶς, μὴ βουλόμενός τινας ἀπολέσθαι ἀλλὰ πάντας εἰς μετάνοιαν χωρῆσαι.

οὐ βραδύνει κύριος τῆς ἐπαγγελίας. Lit. "the Lord of the promise does not delay."
βραδύνει. Pres act ind 3rd sg βραδύνω. Only here and in 1 Tim 3:15 in the NT: "hesitate, delay" (BDAG, 183).
κύριος. Nominative subject of βραδύνει. While this is anarthrous in all of the older manuscripts, as is fitting in a paragraph with hardly an article in it, 𝔐 reads ὁ κύριος.
τῆς ἐπαγγελίας. Genitive of reference ("the Lord is not delaying with respect to the promise"), attributive genitive ("the Lord who promised is not delaying"), or possibly genitive of separation ("the Lord is not holding back, delaying the fulfillment of his promise"; BDF §180.5).
ὥς. Comparitive.
τινες. Nominative subject of ἡγοῦνται.
βραδύτητα. Accusative direct object of ἡγοῦνται. The noun βραδύτης ("slowness") is a NT *hapax legomenon*.
ἡγοῦνται. Pres mid ind 3rd pl ἡγέομαι.
ἀλλά. MHT (4:141) cites this (as also in 1:21) as an example of 2 Peter's tendency to parataxis, thus a weakness in style, although 2 Peter usually relies upon the all-purpose δέ.
μακροθυμεῖ. Pres act ind 3rd sg μακροθυμέω.

εἰς ὑμᾶς. Reference. Some manuscripts (𝔐 *pc*) read εἰς ἡμᾶς ("toward us"), while others (ℵ A Ψ 33 *al*) read δι ὑμᾶς ("on your account"). The NA²⁷/UBS⁴ text, following 𝔓⁷² B C P *al*, has the slightly more difficult and better supported reading.

βουλόμενός. Pres pass ptc masc nom sg βούλομαι (causal).

τινας. Accusative subject of ἀπολέσθαι.

ἀπολέσθαι. Aor mid inf ἀπόλλυμι (complementary).

πάντας. Accusative subject of ἀπολέσθαι.

εἰς μετάνοιαν. Goal.

χωρῆσαι. Aor act inf χωρέω (complementary with an implied βουλόμενος). This verb occurs 10 times in the NT with a range of meanings. Here, it means "to reach" (BDAG, 1094.1.b).

2 Peter 3:10-13

¹⁰But the Day of the Lord will come as a thief (comes), on which (Day) the heavens will pass away with a roar and the heavenly bodies, being burned up, will be destroyed, and the earth and the deeds (done) in it will be exposed. ¹¹Since all these things are thus being destroyed, what sort of people should you be—in holy lifestyles and pious acts—¹²(your ought to be those) expecting and speeding up the coming of the Day of God, because of which the heavens will be destroyed by being set on fire, and the heavenly bodies will dissolve by being burned up. ¹³But we seek the "new heaven and new earth" according to his promise, (a heaven and earth) in which righteousness makes its home.

This subparagraph starts with the destruction of the heavens, and then draws out the consequences with a repetition of a passive form of λύω (two futures and one present) in each verse until the final one, which restores what was destroyed in verse 10. It is characterized by the same type of anarthrous nouns that were seen toward the end of the previous paragraph.

3:10 Ἥξει δὲ ἡμέρα κυρίου ὡς κλέπτης, ἐν ᾗ οἱ οὐρανοὶ ῥοιζηδὸν παρελεύσονται στοιχεῖα δὲ καυσούμενα λυθήσεται καὶ γῆ καὶ τὰ ἐν αὐτῇ ἔργα εὑρεθήσεται.

With five verbal forms in a single verse, four of them future, the author creates a picture of intense activity. Structurally, this sentence consists of a main clause with an implied adverbial clause of manner (ὡς κλέπτης) and a compound relative clause (ἐν ᾗ ... δὲ ... καὶ). The latter structure is significant because different verbal actions affect the different parts of the universe.

Ἥξει. Fut act ind 3rd sg ἥκω.

ἡμέρα κυρίου. Nominative subject of Ἥξει. The expression is anarthrous in 𝔓⁷² B C *al*, but one finds ἡ ἡμέρα κυρίου in ℵ A 𝔐. It is a difficult call textually, for although κύριος is often anarthrous, functioning much like a proper noun (MHT, 3:174), that is not normally true of ἡμέρα. One could easily explain the absence an article before ἡμέρα as haplography, since in an uncial manuscript one would have two ἡ in a row without a space. However, BDF (§259.1) points out that stock phrases like ἡμέρα κυρίου are often anarthrous due to Semitic influence, and this is probably what has influenced the choice of reading in this text.

ὡς. Comparitive.

κλέπτης. Nominative subject of an implied "comes."

ἐν ᾗ. Temporal.

οἱ οὐρανοὶ. Nominative subject of παρελεύσονται.

ῥοιζηδὸν. This adverb is a NT *hapax legomenon* referring to "noise made by something passing with great force and rapidity, *with a rushing noise*" (BDAG, 907).

παρελεύσονται. Fut mid ind 3rd pl παρέρχομαι.

στοιχεῖα. Nominative subject of λυθήσεται. Forms of στοιχεῖον occur seven times in the NT, twice in Gal 4, twice in Col 2, once in Heb 5:12, and twice here. There are four possible meanings: (1) "substances underlying the natural world, the basic *elements*" (usually earth, air, fire, and water); (2) "basic components of celestial constellations, *heavenly bodies*"; (3) "things that constitute the foundation of learning, *fundamental principles*"; and (4) "transcendent powers that are in control over events in this world, *elements, elemental spirits*" (BDAG, 946; cf. Delling, "στοιχέω, συστοιχέω, στοιχεῖον," 666–87). Meaning (2) is most likely here, since this passage is almost certainly dependent on LXX Isa 34:4

and this meaning is clearly found, e.g., in Theophilus of Antioch, *Autol.* 1.4; Justin, *2 Apol.* 5.2; *Dial.* 23.2. For further rationale, see Davids 2006, 283–86.

καυσούμενα. Pres pass ptc neut nom pl καυσόω (means). This contract verb (on the form, see MHT, 2:393–95; cf. MHT, 2:242 on the parsing) is a NT *hapax legomenon* meaning to "be consumed by heat, burn up" (BDAG, 536) either in terms of combustion or in terms of fever.

λυθήσεται. Fut pass ind 3rd sg λύω.

γῆ. Nominative subject of εὑρεθήσεται. The anarthrous form of this noun predominates in the NT (BDF §253.3; so also MHT, 3:174).

εὑρεθήσεται. Fut pass ind 3rd sg εὑρίσκω. There is considerable textual uncertainty about this verb. The NA²⁷/UBS⁴ text is found in ℵ B K P *al*, while 𝔓⁷² adds λυόμενα to parallel what happens to the earth with what happens to the στοιχεῖα. Later manuscripts (A L 𝔐 *pm*), however, read κατακαήσεται (from κατακαίω, "destroy by fire, burn [up], consume by fire"; Friberg, 218; on the form of the verb, see BDF §76), while C has ἀφανισθήσονται (from ἀφανίζω, "perish, disappear"). It is clear that εὑρεθήσεται is the oldest reading, and that "in view of the difficulty of extracting any acceptable sense from the passage, it is not strange that copyists and translators introduced a variety of modifications" (Metzger, 636). Contrary to Metzger, however, there is an acceptable sense that can be derived from the oldest reading in that the main point of both this and the larger passage is the judgment of the ungodly and, especially in the ancient worldview, with the heavens and the heavenly bodies out of the way the earth, along with all done in it, would be "exposed" to the divine "eye" (see further Davids 2006, 286).

3:11 Τούτων οὕτως πάντων λυομένων ποταποὺς δεῖ ὑπάρχειν [ὑμᾶς] ἐν ἁγίαις ἀναστροφαῖς καὶ εὐσεβείαις,

The sentence draws a conclusion using a genitive absolute phrase as a transition.

Τούτων ... πάντων. Genitive subject of λυομένων.

οὕτως. Adverb of manner. While οὕτως πάντων is read by 𝔓⁷⁴ᵛⁱᵈ

B *al* and οὕτως πάντως is found in 𝔓⁷², many manuscripts (ℵ A Ψ 048 𝔐) read οὖν πάντων. Despite the widespread evidence for οὖν πάντων, the combination of the ancient witnesses in B and 𝔓⁷² (the πάντως being an error due to repeating the ending of οὕτως) and the fact that οὖν seems to smooth the somewhat sharp transition has led to the choice in the NA²⁷/UBS⁴ text (see Metzger, 636).

λυομένων. Pres pass ptc neut gen pl λύω. Genitive absolute, causal.

ποταποὺς. Accusative predicate of ὑπάρχειν. This interrogative pronoun refers to quality ("what sort of" or "what kind of"; see BDF §298.3; MHT, 3:48).

δεῖ. Pres act ind 3rd sg δεῖ. This impersonal verb expresses inevitability, necessity, compulsion, obligation, propriety (Friberg, 104).

ὑπάρχειν. Pres act inf ὑπάρχω (complementary).

[ὑμᾶς]. Accusative subject of ὑπάρχειν. The text is uncertain with the NA²⁷/UBS⁴ following 𝔓⁷²ᶜ ℵᶜ A C Ψ 𝔐 *pm*. Some important manuscripts (𝔓⁷²* 𝔓⁷⁴ B *pc*), however, omit the pronoun, while a few others (ℵ *pc*) read ἡμᾶς. This last reading is produced by itacism and is less suitable to the context. The omission of the pronoun, on the other hand, could be an error or "scribal pruning" of a superfluous word. It also, however, makes good sense and is found in very ancient manuscripts. It thus could be original, though the weight of the manuscript evidence is against it; thus the brackets (see Metzger, 637).

ἐν ἁγίαις ἀναστροφαῖς καὶ εὐσεβείαις. Manner. The PP appears to be epexegetical to ποταποὺς, "what sort of people should you be—namely in holy lifestyles and pious acts." Less likely, it could be reference: "what sort of people should you be—with respect to holy lifestyles and pious acts." It could also possibly be taken as manner with the following προσδοκῶντας: "what sort of people should you be—waiting with holy lifestyles and pious acts and...." The plural of ἀναστροφή indicates a variety of holy lifestyles (cf. BDAG, 73), while the plural of εὐσέβεια indicates pious acts or "godly acts" (BDAG, 412). The reference to εὐσέβεια, which is one of the virtues of 1:6, creates a terminological *inclusio* as the work moves toward its conclusion.

3:12 προσδοκῶντας καὶ σπεύδοντας τὴν παρουσίαν τῆς τοῦ θεοῦ ἡμέρας δι' ἣν οὐρανοὶ πυρούμενοι λυθήσονται καὶ στοιχεῖα καυσούμενα τήκεται.

προσδοκῶντας. Pres act ptc masc acc pl προσδοκάω. The participle could be substantival, with the accusative case stemming from the fact that the participle modifies an infinitive, which takes an accusative subject (see Culy 2003, 446, n. 34), or attendant circumstance ("as you wait for and hasten"; cf. NRSV). This verb means "to give thought to something that is viewed as lying in the future, *wait for, look for, expect*" (BDAG, 877).

σπεύδοντας. Pres act ptc masc acc pl σπεύδω (substantival or attendant circumstance; see also above on προσδοκῶντας). This verb occurs six times in the NT, with all other occurrences being in Luke-Acts. While the verb can simply mean "to be in a hurry, *hurry, hasten*" when followed by an infinitive or the preposition πρός, in this passage it is used transitively with an object (τὴν παρουσίαν) and so means "to cause something to happen or come into being by exercising special effort" (BDAG, 938.2).

τὴν παρουσίαν. Accusative direct object of προσδοκῶντας καὶ σπεύδοντας.

τῆς ... ἡμέρας. Subjective genitive.

τοῦ θεοῦ. Possessive genitive.

δι' ἣν. Causal.

οὐρανοὶ. Nominative subject of λυθήσονται.

πυρούμενοι. Pres pass ptc masc nom pl πυρόω (means). This verb occurs six times in the NT, meaning in most cases "to cause to be on fire, burn," either literally or figuratively (BDAG, 899).

λυθήσονται. Fut pass ind 3rd pl λύω.

καυσούμενα. Pres pass ptc neut nom pl καυσόω (means). This verb is a NT *hapax legomenon* meaning "be consumed by heat, burn up" (BDAG, 536).

τήκεται. Pres pass ind 3rd sg τήκω. This verb is a NT *hapax legomenon* meaning "to cause something to become liquid, melt," and thus in the passive voice, "melt, dissolve" (BDAG, 1001). On the form, see MHT, 2:261.

3:13 καινοὺς δὲ οὐρανοὺς καὶ γῆν καινὴν κατὰ τὸ ἐπάγγελμα αὐτοῦ προσδοκῶμεν, ἐν οἷς δικαιοσύνη κατοικεῖ.

The paragraph concludes with a repetition of the verb προσδοκάω, with a quotation from LXX Isa 65:17//Isa 66:22 functioning as the direct object, which is fronted for emphasis, and a final relative clause describing these new or renewed entities.

καινοὺς . . . οὐρανοὺς καὶ γῆν καινὴν. Accusative direct object of προσδοκῶμεν. Fronted for emphasis. Unlike the LXX, 2 Peter does not use the article with οὐρανός or γῆ, which is a common practice, especially with οὐρανός, in both this chapter and NT Greek in general (BDF §253.3).

κατὰ τὸ ἐπάγγελμα. Standard. The noun ἐπάγγελμα ("promise") is used in the NT only here and in 1:4, with the two occurrences forming an *inclusio*. Some copyists (א A Ψ *pc*) conform this reference to the plural in 1:4, reading ἐπαγγέλματα. The majority of manuscripts have the singular form, which fits well with the one promise quoted from Isaiah.

αὐτοῦ. Subjective genitive.

προσδοκῶμεν. Pres act ind 1st pl προσδοκάω. This is an example of the inclusive "we" (Wallace, 398).

ἐν οἷς. Locative.

δικαιοσύνη. Nominative subject of κατοικεῖ.

κατοικεῖ. Pres act ind 3rd sg κατοικέω.

2 Peter 3:14-16

[14]Therefore, loved ones, since you expect these things, make every effort to be found uncorrupted and blameless in his estimation, in peace. [15]And consider our Lord's long-suffering (to be) salvation, as also our beloved brother Paul has written to you, according to the wisdom given to him, [16]as (he writes) in all (his) letters, when he speaks in them concerning these things. In them some things are hard to understand, which the unlearned and unstable distort to their own destruction, as (they) also (do) the rest of the Scriptures.

Both Διό and the vocative indicate that a new paragraph has begun, this one consisting of one long complex sentence.

3:14 Διό, ἀγαπητοί, ταῦτα προσδοκῶντες σπουδάσατε ἄσπιλοι καὶ ἀμώμητοι αὐτῷ εὑρεθῆναι ἐν εἰρήνῃ

ἀγαπητοί. Vocative.
ταῦτα. Accusative direct object of προσδοκῶντες.
προσδοκῶντες. Pres act ptc masc nom pl προσδοκάω (causal or temporal, "as you wait for").
σπουδάσατε. Aor act impv 2nd pl σπουδάζω.
ἄσπιλοι καὶ ἀμώμητοι. Complement in a subject-complement double nominative construction (see Culy 2009, 85–87). The alliterative adjectival pair is unique in the NT. ἀμώμητοι ("blameless, without reproach"; Friberg, 47) is a NT *hapax legomenon*, while ἄσπιλοι ("spotless, without defect" in the literal sense, "pure, clean, uncorrupted" in the moral sense; Friberg, 79) appears only four times in the NT (also 1 Tim 6:14; Jas 1:27; 1 Pet 1:19). Perhaps because ἄμωμοι ("unblemished" when used of sacrifices, "blameless, without fault" when used in the moral sense; Friberg, 47) is more common than ἀμώμητοι (it appears 10 times in the NT) and is paired with ἄσπιλοι in 1 Pet 1:19, some manuscripts (A 33 *al*) read it instead of ἀμώμητοι.
αὐτῷ. Ethical dative (MHT, 3:239; BDF §192; cf. Wallace, 147), or dative of agency, "to be found by him uncorrupted and blameless."
εὑρεθῆναι. Aor pass inf εὑρίσκω (complementary).
ἐν εἰρήνῃ. This PP represents a second complement in the infinitive clause. Here, the preposition should likely be viewed as a "marker of a state or condition" (BDAG 327.2). It is unclear whether the "peace" relates to other people, to God, or both.

3:15 καὶ τὴν τοῦ κυρίου ἡμῶν μακροθυμίαν σωτηρίαν ἡγεῖσθε, καθὼς καὶ ὁ ἀγαπητὸς ἡμῶν ἀδελφὸς Παῦλος κατὰ τὴν δοθεῖσαν αὐτῷ σοφίαν ἔγραψεν ὑμῖν,

Here, the second main clause of the sentence begun in the previous verse is followed by an adverbial clause that will be further modified in the following verse. Wallace (8) notes verses 15-16 as an example of the cryptic nature of language.

τὴν ... μακροθυμίαν. Accusative direct object of ἡγεῖσθε.
τοῦ κυρίου. Subjective genitive.
ἡμῶν. Genitive of subordination.
σωτηρίαν. Complement in an object-complement double accusative construction.
ἡγεῖσθε. Pres mid impv 2nd pl ἡγέομαι.
καθώς. Introduces a comparative adverbial clause of manner.
ὁ ἀγαπητὸς ... ἀδελφὸς. Nominative subject of ἔγραψεν.
ἡμῶν. Genitive of relationship.
Παῦλος. Nominative in apposition to ὁ ἀγαπητὸς ... ἀδελφὸς.
κατὰ τὴν ... σοφίαν. Standard.
δοθεῖσαν. Aor pass ptc fem acc sg δίδωμι (attributive).
αὐτῷ. Dative indirect object of δοθεῖσαν.
ἔγραψεν. Aor act ind 3rd sg γράφω.
ὑμῖν. Dative indirect object of ἔγραψεν.

3:16 ὡς καὶ ἐν πάσαις ἐπιστολαῖς λαλῶν ἐν αὐταῖς περὶ τούτων, ἐν αἷς ἐστιν δυσνόητά τινα, ἃ οἱ ἀμαθεῖς καὶ ἀστήρικτοι στρεβλοῦσιν ὡς καὶ τὰς λοιπὰς γραφὰς πρὸς τὴν ἰδίαν αὐτῶν ἀπώλειαν.

A final comparative adverbial clause (ὡς καὶ), followed by two relative clauses, the final one of which is modified by another adverbial clause, completes the sentence and the paragraph.

ὡς. Introduces a comparative clause.
ἐν πάσαις ἐπιστολαῖς. Locative. BDF (§275.1) reads πάσαις ταῖς ἐπιστολαῖς with ℵ P 𝔐 against 𝔓⁷² A B C Ψ 33 *al* on grammatical grounds. Given, however, that the article is common after πᾶς, it could easily have been unconsciously added by a later copiest.
λαλῶν. Pres act ptc masc nom sg λαλέω (temporal, modifying an implied γράφει).
ἐν αὐταῖς. Locative.
περὶ τούτων. Reference.
ἐν αἷς. Locative.
ἐστιν. Pres act ind 3rd sg εἰμί.
δυσνόητά. Predicate adjective. The verbal adjective δυσνόητος

("hard to understand"; BDAG, 265) is a NT *hapax legomenon*. On its formation, see BDF §117.1.

τινα. Nominative subject of ἐστιν.

ἅ. Accusative direct object of στρεβλοῦσιν.

οἱ ἀμαθεῖς καὶ ἀστήρικτοι. Nominative subject of στρεβλοῦσιν. The term ἀμαθής is a NT *hapax legomenon* and refers to someone who is "unlearned, ignorant, uneducated." Here, in its substantival form it refers to "untaught people" (Friberg, 45). The term ἀστήρικτος appears only twice in the NT (also 2:14) and means "unstable, weak" (BDAG, 145).

στρεβλοῦσιν. Pres act ind 3rd pl στρεβλόω. A NT *hapax legomenon* meaning "to distort a statement so that a false meaning results, *twist, distort*" (BDAG 948).

τὰς λοιπὰς γραφάς. Accusative direct object of an implied στρεβλοῦσιν.

πρὸς τὴν ἰδίαν . . . ἀπώλειαν. Result. The adjective ἴδιος is reflexive here (MHT, 3:192; BDF §286.1, point to this as a classical usage). This usage was not picked up by the scribe of 𝔓⁷² who changed αὐτῶν to ἑαυτῶν.

αὐτῶν. Objective genitive.

2 Peter 3:17-18

¹⁷You, therefore, loved ones, since you know this in advance, be on your guard so that you do not fall from your own state of security, being carried away by the error of the disgraceful, ¹⁸but grow in the grace and knowledge of our Lord and Savior, Jesus the Anointed One. To whom be glory, both now and until the Day of Eternity. Amen.

The final paragraph is marked off by οὖν and a repetition of the direct address to the readers (Ὑμεῖς . . . ἀγαπητοί). It consists of a single compound sentence followed by a nominal clause that is a doxology.

3:17 Ὑμεῖς οὖν, ἀγαπητοί, προγινώσκοντες φυλάσσεσθε, ἵνα μὴ τῇ τῶν ἀθέσμων πλάνῃ συναπαχθέντες ἐκπέσητε τοῦ ἰδίου στηριγμοῦ,

Ὑμεῖς. Nominative subject of φυλάσσεσθε.
ἀγαπητοί. Vocative.
προγινώσκοντες. Pres act ptc nom masc pl προγινώσκω (causal). This verb is used only five times in the NT and here means "to know beforehand or in advance, have foreknowledge" (BDAG, 866.1).
φυλάσσεσθε. Pres mid impv 2nd pl φυλάσσω.
ἵνα. Introduces a (negative) purpose clause.
τῇ ... πλάνῃ. Dative of instrument. The adjective ἄθεσμος is found in the NT only here and in 2:7 and means "pertaining to being unprincipled, unseemly, disgraceful, lawless" (BDAG, 24).
τῶν ἀθέσμων. Subjective genitive. Only here and in 2:7 in the NT: "being unprincipled, *unseemly, disgraceful, lawless*" (BDAG, 24).
συναπαχθέντες. Aor pass ptc masc nom pl συναπάγω (attendant circumstance or causal, "because you are carried way by the error..."). This verb is used three times in the NT (also Rom 12:16; Gal 2:13) and here means "to cause someone in conjunction with others to go astray in belief" (BDAG, 965).
ἐκπέσητε. Aor act subj 2nd pl ἐκπίπτω. Subjunctive with ἵνα. This verb appears 10 times in the NT meaning literally "to fall from some point, fall" or nautically "to drift or be blown off course and run aground." Here, the sense is "to change for the worse from a favorable condition" (BDAG, 308.3).
τοῦ ἰδίου στηριγμοῦ. Genitive of separation. BDF (§181) views this genitive as "more or less dependent" on the prepositional prefix ἐκ- in ἐκπέσητε. The noun στηριγμός is a NT *hapax legomenon* meaning "state of security, safe position" or "firm commitment to conviction or belief" (BDAG, 945). Here, ἴδιος is a reflexive adjective.

3:18 αὐξάνετε δὲ ἐν χάριτι καὶ γνώσει τοῦ κυρίου ἡμῶν καὶ σωτῆρος Ἰησοῦ Χριστοῦ. αὐτῷ ἡ δόξα καὶ νῦν καὶ εἰς ἡμέραν αἰῶνος. [ἀμήν.]

αὐξάνετε. Pres act impv 2nd pl αὐξάνω.
ἐν χάριτι καὶ γνώσει. Reference.

τοῦ κυρίου... καὶ σωτῆρος. These nouns likely relate to χάριτι as a genitive of source ("grace from the Lord and Savior") and to γνώσει as either a genitive of source ("knowledge from the Lord and Savior") or more likely an objective genitive ("knowledge about the Lord and Savior"). Following the Granville-Sharp Rule the two nouns refer to a single referent (see Wallace, 274; cf. Wallace, 223; BDF §276.3).

ἡμῶν. Genitive of subordination.

Ἰησοῦ Χριστοῦ. Genitive in apposition to τοῦ κυρίου... καὶ σωτῆρος. See also Jude 1 on Χριστοῦ.

αὐτῷ. Dative of possession. See also Jude 24 on Τῷ... δυναμένῳ.

ἡ δόξα. Nominative subject of an implied verb. See Jude 25.

καὶ... καὶ. This construction means "both... and" or "not only... but also" (BDAG, 495).

εἰς ἡμέραν αἰῶνος. An idiom (lit. "to the day of the age") meaning "forever" or "to eternity" (BDAG, 32.1.b, s.v. αἰών)

[ἀμήν.] This particle is present in $\mathfrak{P}^{72}$ ℵ A C P Ψ 𝔐 but missing in B *pc*. It could have been added to the majority because it was a standard ending of doxologies. Thus the brackets express doubt on the part of the editors of the NA^{27}/UBS^4, despite very strong early manuscript support (Metzger, 637).

GLOSSARY

Anacolouthon — A construction involving some sort of break in grammatical sequence.

Anarthrous — Lacking an article.

Antecedent — An element that is referred to by another expression that follows it. Thus, the antecedent of a relative pronoun is that element in the preceding context to which the relative clause provides additional information.

Apodosis — The second part ("then" clause) in a conditional construction.

Aposiopesis — A sudden break in the midst of a sentence, often implying an inability or unwillingness to proceed.

Articular — Including an article.

Ascensive — In Greek, this term is most often used in relation to conjunctions, especially καί. It refers to a usage that is intensive or expresses a final addition or point of focus. In such instances, the conjunction is typically translated, "even."

Aspect — This term is used in relation to verb tense and refers to the writer's/speaker's subjective choice of how to portray the verbal action, e.g., perfective or imperfective.

Attraction — Relative pronouns at times take on or "attract" to the case of their antecedent. For example, in the text, Πάντων δὲ θαυμαζόντων ἐπὶ πᾶσιν οἷς ἐποίει εἶπεν πρὸς τοὺς μαθητὰς αὐτοῦ ("While everyone was marveling at all that he was doing, he said to his disciples"), the expected case for the relative pronoun would be accusative (οὕς), since it functions as the direct object of ἐποίει. Instead, it has been attracted to the case of its antecedent (πᾶσιν).

Causative — Causative verbs or constructions denote that a new state of affairs is brought about or "caused" by the action of the verb or construction. Both δίδωμι and ποιέω are examples of verbs that can be used to form a causative construction. For example, in the text, δὸς τοῖς δούλοις σου μετὰ παρρησίας πάσης λαλεῖν τὸν λόγον σου (lit. "Give to your servants to speak your word with all boldness") the imperative and infinitive verbs (δὸς and λαλεῖν) form a causative verb phrase ("cause to speak").

Clausal complement — This type of complement is structurally a direct object, but since it is a clause rather than a noun phrase scholars often use the language of "complement" rather than "direct object." For example, ὅτι is often used to introduce complement clauses with verbs of speech that represent what was said: λέγω γὰρ ὑμῖν ὅτι δύναται ὁ θεὸς ἐκ τῶν λίθων τούτων ἐγεῖραι τέκνα τῷ Ἀβραάμ ("For I tell you that God is able to raise up children for Abraham from these stones.")

Complement — In the handbook, this term is used in two ways in addition to its use in the phrase, "clausal complement": (1) A constituent, other than an accusative direct object, that is required to complete a verb phrase. Verbs that include a prepositional prefix often take a complement whose case is determined by the prefix. For example, verbs with the prefix συν- characteristically take a dative complement. (2) The second element in a double accusative construction, which completes the verbal idea. In the sentence, "I call my son Superman," Superman would be the complement.

Constructio ad sensum — Lit. "construction according to sense." A construction that follows the sense of the expression rather than strict grammatical rules, e.g., the use of a plural verb with a subject that is syntactically singular but refers to a group of people.

Dittography — The accidental repetition of text.

Equative verb/clause — An equative verb, like εἰμί, γίνομαι, or ὑπάρχω, is a verb that joins a subject and predicate to form an equative clause ("something is something"), e.g., Ἡ γενεὰ αὕτη γενεὰ πονηρά ἐστιν ("This generation is a wicked generation").

Fronting — Placing a constituent earlier in the sentence than its default order, most commonly in a pre-verbal position.

Genitive of relationship — Wallace (83) prefers to limit this label to familial relationships, but we have followed Young (25-26) in applying it to a variety of social relationships as well, including slaves, friends, and enemies.

Hapax legomenon — A word that occurs only one time in the NT or in a designated body of literature.

Haplography — The accidental omission of text.

Inclusio — An "envelope" or "bookend" structure in which the same or similar language is used to begin and end a unit of discourse.

Left-dislocation — This literary device introduces "the next primary topic of the discourse" (Runge §14.2) by placing it at the beginning of the sentence and then picking it up with a resumptive pronoun in the actual sentence. For example, "The struggling student in my Greek class, he passed his mid-term exam with flying colors."

Nominal (clause) — A nominal is a noun or something that functions like a noun. In a nominal clause, a nominative noun stands alone in the clause without a verb, and sometimes without any other elements.

Pleonastic — Redundant or superfluous.

Polyptoton — The repetition of a word, related word, or syntactic form within the same sentence for rhetorical effect.

Protasis — The first part ("if" clause) in a conditional construction.

Solitarium — The phrase, τε *solitarium*, refers to the use of τε without an accompanying conjunction, such as καί.

Tautology — An unnecessary repetition of material that is readily available in the immediate context.

BIBLIOGRAPHY

Abbott, Edwin A. *Johannine Grammar*. London: Cambridge University Press, 1906.

_____. *Johannine Vocabulary*. London: Adam & Charles Black, 1905.

Aland, Barbara et al. *Novum Testamentum Graecum Edition Critica Maior*. IV Catholic Letters Installment 2. Stuttgart: Deutsche Bibelgesellschaft, 2000.

Bakker, Egbert J. "Voice, Aspect and Aktionsart: Middle and Passive in Ancient Greek." Pages 23–47 in *Voice: Form and Function. Typological Studies in Language* 27. Edited by B. A. Fox and P. J. Hopper. Philadelphia: John Benjamins, 1994.

Bauckham, Richard J. *2 Peter, Jude*. Word Biblical Commentary 50. Dallas: Word, 2002.

Bauer, Walter, William F. Arndt, F. Wilbur Gingrich, and Frederick W. Danker. *A Greek-English Lexicon of the New Testament and Other Early Christian Literature*. 3rd ed. Chicago: University of Chicago Press, 2000.

Bigg, Charles. *The Epistles of St. Peter and St. Jude*. International Critical Commentary. Edinburgh: T&T Clark, 1901.

Blass, F., and A. Debrunner. *A Greek Grammar of the New Testament and Other Early Christian Literature*. Translated and revised by Robert W. Funk. Chicago: University of Chicago Press, 1961.

Bovon, François. *Luke 1: A Commentary on the Gospel of Luke 1:1–9:50*. Hermeneia. Translated by C. M. Thomas. Minneapolis: Augsburg Fortress, 2002.

Bultmann, R. "πιστεύω." Pages 173–277 in vol. 6 of *Theological Dictionary of the New Testament*. Edited by G. Kittel and G.

Friedrich. Translated by G. Bromiley. 10 vols. Grand Rapids: Eerdmans, 1964–1976.

Büchsel, Friedrich. "κρίνω, κρίσις, κτλ." Pages 921–54 in vol. 3 of *Theological Dictionary of the New Testament*. Edited by G. Kittel and G. Friedrich. Translated by G. Bromiley. 10 vols. Grand Rapids: Eerdmans, 1964–1976.

Caragounis, Chrys C. *The Development of Greek and the New Testament: Morphology, Syntax, Phonology, and Textual Transmission*. Grand Rapids: Baker Academic, 2006.

Charles, J. Daryl. *Literary Strategy in the Epistle of Jude*. Scranton, Pa.: University of Scranton Press, 1993.

Chester, Andrew, and Ralph P. Martin. *The Theology of the Letters of James, Peter, and Jude*. New Testament Theology. Cambridge: Cambridge University Press, 1994.

Conrad, Carl W. "New Observations on Voice in the Ancient Greek Verb. November 19, 2002." Online: http://artsci.wustl.edu/~cwconrad/docs/NewObsAncGrkVc.pdf. Accessed June 8, 2009.

Culy, Martin M. "The Clue is in the Case: Distinguishing Adjectival and Adverbial Participles." *Perspectives in Religious Studies* 30 (2003): 441–53.

———. "Double Case Constructions in Koine Greek." *Journal of Greco-Roman Christianity and Judaism* 6 (2009): 82–106.

Culy, Martin M., and Mikeal C. Parsons. *Acts: A Handbook on the Greek Text*. Baylor Handbook on the Greek New Testament. Waco, Tex.: Baylor University Press, 2003.

Culy, Martin M., Mikeal C. Parsons, and Joshua J. Stigall. *Luke: A Handbook on the Greek Text*. Baylor Handbook on the Greek New Testament. Waco, Tex.: Baylor University Press, 2010.

Davids, Peter H. "The Catholic Epistles as a Canonical Janus." *Bulletin for Biblical Research* 19.3 (2009): 403–16.

———. *The Letters of 2 Peter and Jude*. The Pillar New Testament Commentary. Grand Rapids: Eerdmans, 2006.

———. "The Use of Second Temple Traditions in 1 and 2 Peter and Jude." Pages 409–31 in *The Catholic Epistles and the Tradition*.

Edited by Jacques Schlosser. Bibliotheca Ephemeridum Theologicarum Lovaniensium 176. Leuven: Peeters, 2004.

———. *More Hard Sayings of the New Testament.* Downers Grove, Ill.: InterVarsity, 1991.

Delling, Gerhard. "στοιχέω, συστοιχέω, στοιχεῖον." Pages 666–87 in vol. 7 of *Theological Dictionary of the New Testament.* Edited by G. Kittel and G. Friedrich. Translated by G. Bromiley. 10 vols. Grand Rapids: Eerdmans, 1964–1976.

———. "τρεῖς, τρίς, τρίτος." Pages 216–25 in vol. 8 of *Theological Dictionary of the New Testament.* Edited by G. Kittel and G. Friedrich. Translated by G. Bromiley. 10 vols. Grand Rapids: Eerdmans, 1964–1976.

Friberg, Timothy, Barbara Friberg, and Neva F. Miller. *Analytical Lexicon of the Greek New Testament.* Grand Rapids: Baker, 2000.

Green, Gene L. *Jude & 2 Peter.* Baker Exegetical Commentary on the New Testament. Grand Rapids: Baker, 2008.

Hauck, Friedrich. "μῶμος, ἄμωμος, ἀμώμητος." Pages 829–31 in vol. 4 of *Theological Dictionary of the New Testament.* Edited by G. Kittel and G. Friedrich. Translated by G. Bromiley. 10 vols. Grand Rapids: Eerdmans, 1964–1976.

Kelly, John Normal Davidson. *A Commentary on the Epistles of Peter and Jude.* Black's New Testament Commentaries. Grand Rapids: Baker, 1981.

Kemmer, Suzanne. *The Middle Voice.* Philadelphia: John Benjamins, 1993.

Kittel, Gerhard, and Gerhard Friedrich, eds. *Theological Dictionary of the New Testament.* Translated by G. Bromiley. 10 vols. Grand Rapids: Eerdmans, 1964–1976.

Kraftchick, Steven J. *Jude, 2 Peter.* Abingdon New Testament Commentaries. Nashville: Abingdon, 2002.

Kraus, Thomas J. *Sprache, Stil und historischer Ort des zweiten Petrusbriefes.* Wissenschaftliche Untersuchungen zum Neuen Testament 2.136. Tübingen: Mohr Siebeck, 2001.

Landon, Charles. *A Text-Critical Study of the Epistle of Jude.* Journal for the Study of the New Testament: Supplement Series 135. Sheffield: Sheffield Academic Press, 1996.

Levinsohn, Stephen H. *Discourse Features of New Testament Greek: A Coursebook on the Information Structure of New Testament Greek*. 2nd ed. Dallas: SIL, 2000.

Lukaszewski, Albert L. *The Lexham Syntactic Greek New Testament: Expansions and Annotations*. Bellingham, Wash.: Logos Research Systems, 2006.

Marshall, I. Howard. *The Gospel of Luke: A Commentary on the Greek Text*. New International Greek Testament Commentary. Grand Rapids: Eerdmans, 1978.

Metzger, Bruce M. *A Textual Commentary on the Greek New Testament*. 2nd ed. Stuttgart: Deutsche Bibelgesellschaft, 1994.

Michel, Otto. "οἶκος, οἰκία, κτλ." Pages 119–59 in vol. 5 of *Theological Dictionary of the New Testament*. Edited by G. Kittel and G. Friedrich. Translated by G. Bromiley. 10 vols. Grand Rapids: Eerdmans, 1964–1976.

Miller, Neva F. "Appendix 2: A Theory of Deponent Verbs." Pages 423–30 in *Analytical Lexicon of the Greek New Testament*. Edited by T. Friberg, B. Friberg, and N. Miller. Grand Rapids: Baker, 2000.

Moulton, James Hope, Wilbert Francis Howard, and Nigel Turner. *A Grammar of New Testament Greek*. 4 vols. Edinburgh: T&T Clark, 1908–1976.

Mounce, William D. *The Morphology of Biblical Greek*. Grand Rapids: Zondervan, 1994.

Neyrey, Jerome H. *2 Peter, Jude: A New Translation with Introduction and Commentary*. Anchor Bible. New York: Doubleday, 1993.

Penner, Ken, and Michael S. Heiser. *Old Testament Greek Pseudepigrapha with Morphology*. Bellingham, Wash.: Logos Research Systems, 2008.

Pennington, Jonathan T. "Deponency in Koine Greek: The Grammatical Question and the Lexicographical Dilemma." *Trinity Journal* 24 (2003): 55–76.

Porter, Stanley E. *Idioms of the Greek New Testament*. 2nd ed. Sheffield: Sheffield Academic Press, 1994.

Reese, Ruth Anne. *2 Peter & Jude*. The Two Horizons New Testament Commentary. Grand Rapids: Eerdmans, 2007.

Robertson, A. T. *A Grammar of the Greek New Testament in the Light of Historical Research*. Nashville: Broadman Press, 1934.

Runge, Steven E. A *Discourse Grammar of the Greek New Testament: A Practical Introduction for Teaching and Exegesis*. Bellingham, Wash.: Logos Research Systems, 2010.

Schmidt, Karl Ludwig. "ὁρίζω, ἀφορίζω, κτλ." Pages 452–56 in vol. 5 of Theological Dictionary of the New Testament. Edited by G. Kittel and G. Friedrich. Translated by G. Bromiley. 10 vols. Grand Rapids: Eerdmans, 1964–1976.

Schweizer, Eduard. "ψυχικός." Pages 661–63 in vol. 9 of Theological Dictionary of the New Testament. Edited by G. Kittel and G. Friedrich. Translated by G. Bromiley. 10 vols. Grand Rapids: Eerdmans, 1964–1976.

Stahlin, Gustav. "προσκόπτω, πρόσκομμα, κτλ." Pages 745–58 in vol. 6 of Theological Dictionary of the New Testament. Edited by G. Kittel and G. Friedrich. Translated by G. Bromiley. 10 vols. Grand Rapids: Eerdmans, 1964–1976.

Taylor, Bernard A. "Deponency and Greek Lexicography." Pages 167–76 in *Biblical Greek Language and Lexicography: Essays in Honor of Frederick W. Danker*. Edited by B. A. Taylor et al. Grand Rapids: Eerdmans, 2004.

Towner, Philip H. *The Letters to Timothy and Titus*. New International Commentary on the New Testament. Grand Rapids: Eerdmans, 2006.

Vögtle, Anton. *Der Judasbrief Der Zweite Petrusbrief*. Zürich: Benziger, 1994.

Wallace, Daniel B. *Greek Grammar Beyond the Basics: An Exegetical Syntax of the New Testament*. Grand Rapids: Zondervan, 1996.

Watson, Duane Frederick. *Invention, Arrangement, and Style: Rhetorical Criticism of Jude and 2 Peter*. Society of Biblical Literature Dissertation Series 104. Atlanta: Scholars Press, 1988.

Witherington, Ben III. *Letters and Homilies for Jewish Christians: A Socio-Rhetorical Commentary on Hebrews, James and Jude.* Downers Grove, Ill.: InterVarsity Academic, 2007.

Zerwick, Max, and Mary Grosvenor. *A Grammatical Analysis of the Greek New Testament.* Rome: Biblical Institute Press, 1974.

GRAMMAR INDEX

accusative, adverbial of manner, Jd 7

accusative direct object, Jd 3^2, 4^2, 5^2, 6^3, 7, 8^3, 9, 10^2, 12, 13, 15^2, 19, 20, 21^2, 22, 23^3, 24; 2 Pt 1:1, 3, 4, 5^3, 6^3, 7^2, 9, 10^3, 12, 13, 15, 16^2, 17^2, 18, 19, 20; $2:1^4$, 3, 5^2, 6^2, 7, 8, 9^2, $10a^2$, 10b, 11, 13, 14^3, 15^2, 16^2, 18^3, 19, 20, 21; $3:1^2$, 3, 5, 9, 12, 13^2, 14, 15, 16^2

accusative in apposition, Jd 4, 5; 2 Pt 2:5

accusative neuter, used adverbially, Jd 5

accusative of content, Jd 7

accusative of extent of time, 2 Pt 2:8

accusative of respect, 2 Pt 1:5; 2:11, 13; 3:5, 8

accusative predicate, 2 Pt 3:11

accusative subject of the infinitive, Jd 5; 2 Pt 1:15; 3:9, 11

active voice, Jd 16

adjective (substantival), Jd 3, 4, 18, 19; 2 Pt 3:3

adjective (verbal), Jd 24

adverbial clause, 2 Pt 1:13; 3:10, 16

adverb of degree, 2 Pt 3:3

ἀεί (temporal adverb), 2 Pt 1:12

ἀλλά, Jd 9; 2 Pt 2:1, 5

alliteration, 2 Pt 3:14

alpha privative, Jd 24

ἀμήν, Jd 25; 2 Pt 3:18

anacolouthon, 2 Pt 1:3; 3:3

anarthrous, Jd 18; 2 Pt 2:5, 9, 14; 3:3, 4, 5^2, 9, 10, 13

antecedent, Jd 7; 2 Pt $1:4^2$; 2:12; 3:6

aorist tense, Jd 11, 14; 2 Pt 1:17

ἅπαξ, Jd 3, 5

ἀπό (adverbial conjunctive use), 2 Pt 3:4

ἀπό (agency), Jd 23; 2 Pt 1:21

ἀπό (source), 2 Pt 1:21

ἀπό (temporal), 2 Pt 3:4

apodosis, 2 Pt 2:4, 20

aposiopesis, Jd 22

Asian style (or grand style), 2 Pt 1:5, 15

aspect (imperfective), 2 Pt 2:20

assonance, Jd 15

Attic or classical style, 2 Pt 1:15; 2:4, 5, 7, 19, 21, 22; 3:1, 3, 6, 16

attraction (genitive), Jd 15^2

attraction (nominative), 2 Pt 3:5

attributive use of a correlative adverb of time, 2 Pt 3:6, 7

αὐτός (intensive), 2 Pt 2:19; 3:7

complement in double accusative, Jd 24; 2 Pt 1:8, 10, 13, 19; 2:6, 13; 3:3, 15
complement in double nominative, 2 Pt 3:14
condition (first class), 2 Pt 2:4
constructio ad sensum, Jd 12; 2 Pt 3:1, 5, 6

dative complement, Jd 3; 2 Pt 1:1, 16, 19^2; 2:1, 5, 19, 20
dative complement of a συν-verb, 2 Pt 2:13
dative direct object, Jd 9
dative in apposition, Jd 25^2
dative indirect object, Jd 2, 3^3; 2 Pt 1:2, 4, 14, 16; 2:19, 21; 3:1, 15^2
dative of advantage, Jd 1, 2; 2 Pt 1:2, 11; 2:6, 21
dative of agency, Jd 1; 2 Pt 2:20
dative of cause, 2 Pt 2:8
dative of disadvantage, Jd 9, 11, 13; 2 Pt 2:17, 21
dative of location, Jd 11^3; 2 Pt 1:9; 2:4
dative of means/instrument, Jd 6; 2 Pt 1:3, 21; 2:3, 4, 6, 8^3, 18, 19; 3:3, 5, 6, 7, 17
dative of possession, 2 Pt 1:9; 3:18
dative of purpose, 2 Pt 3:7
dative of recipient, Jd 1; 2 Pt 1:1
dative of reference or respect, Jd 3, 7, 14, 20; 2 Pt 2:2, 3, 11^2, 20, 21
dative of result, 2 Pt 2:6
δέ (developmental marker or copulative), Jd 1, 8, 9, 10, 14, 17, 20, 23^2, 24; 2 Pt 2:1
deponency, 2 Pt 3:4
διά (cause), 2 Pt 2:2; 3:12

διά (intermediate agent), Jd 25; 2 Pt 3:5, 6
διά (means), 2 Pt 1:3^2, 4^2; 3:5
διό (inferential conjunction), 2 Pt 1:10, 12; 3:14
δίς (adverb), Jd 12
dittography, Jd 4, 5, 20, 22; 2 Pt 1:19; 2:21

εἰ (protasis of condition), 2 Pt 2:4, 20
εἰς (direction), Jd 4
εἰς (goal), Jd 4, 6, 21; 2 Pt 1:8; 2:4, 9; 3:7, 9
εἰς (locative), 2 Pt 1:11; 2:22
εἰς (purpose), 2 Pt 2:4, 9, 11; 3:7
εἰς (reference), 2 Pt 1:8, 17; 3:9
εἰς (temporal), Jd 25
ἐκ (means), 2 Pt 3:5
ἐκ (separation), Jd 5, 23; 2 Pt 2:9, 21
ἐκ (source), 2 Pt 1:17; 3:5
ellipsis, 2 Pt 2:10a, 15, 21, 22; 3:4, 5
ἐν (association), Jd 14; 2 Pt 1:5^2, 6^3, 7^2; 2:1, 8
ἐν (cause), 2 Pt 1:2, 4; 2:3, 11
ἐν (condition), 2 Pt 3:14
ἐν (context), 2 Pt 2:11
ἐν (instrumental), Jd 10, 20; 2 Pt 1:1, 2, 4, 13; 2:16, 18, 20; 3:1, 3
ἐν (locative), Jd 1, 12; 2 Pt 1:4, 13, 18, 19; 3:1, 13, 16^3
ἐν (manner), Jd 23, 24; 2 Pt 2:7, 18; 3:11
ἐν (reference), 2 Pt 1:12; 2:7, 11; 3:11, 18
ἐν (sphere), Jd 20, 21; 2 Pt 1:2, 12; 2:13
ἐν (temporal), 2 Pt 2:11, 13; 3:10

ἐπί (locative), 2 Pt 2:22
ἐπί (temporal), Jd 18; 2 Pt 1:13; 3:3
ethical dative, 2 Pt 3:14
ethos, Jd 3, 17
ἕως, 2 Pt 1:19

fronting, Jd 5, 21; 2 Pt 1:1, 4, 18; 2:16; 3:13
future tense, Jd 18; 2 Pt 2:1, 2²

γάρ (causal), Jd 4; 2 Pt 2:18, 19, 21; 3:4
γάρ (explanatory), 2 Pt 1:16, 17, 21; 2:4, 8, 20; 3:5
genitive absolute (cause), 2 Pt 1:3; 3:11
genitive absolute (temporal), 2 Pt 1:17
genitive (attributive), Jd 13²; 2 Pt 2:1, 2, 4, 10a, 14, 15, 17, 18, 21, 22²; 3:9
genitive complement, 2 Pt 1:4; 2:10a
genitive direct object, Jd 17; 2 Pt 2:2, 4, 5; 3:2²
genitive (epexegetical), Jd 5, 7, 9, 11, 13; 2 Pt 2:6, 17
genitive in apposition, Jd 1, 17, 21², 25; 2 Pt 1:1, 2, 8, 11, 14, 16; 2:20; 3:18
genitive (objective), Jd 3, 18, 21, 25; 2 Pt 1:1, 2, 3, 4, 8, 9², 10, 14, 15, 16; 2:3, 5, 6, 12, 16, 19, 20; 3:4, 7, 16, 18
genitive of comparison, 2 Pt 2:20
genitive of content/quality, Jd 11, 15; 2 Pt 2:4, 5, 14
genitive of destination, 2 Pt 2:1

genitive of material, 2 Pt 2:4
genitive of possession, Jd 1, 12, 14; 2 Pt 1:8, 14; 2:16, 19, 20; 3:1, 12
genitive of production/producer, 2 Pt 2:13
genitive of reference, 2 Pt 2:14, 16; 3:9
genitive of relationship, Jd 1; 2 Pt 1:17²; 3:2, 15
genitive of separation, 2 Pt 2:14; 3:9, 17
genitive of source, 2 Pt 1:20²; 2:15, 20; 3:5, 18
genitive of subordination, Jd 4², 17, 21, 25; 2 Pt 1:1, 2, 8, 11, 14, 16; 2:20; 3:15, 18
genitive subject, 2 Pt 1:3, 17; 3:11
genitive (subjective), Jd 4, 15, 17, 20, 21², 24; 2 Pt 1:1², 3, 5, 9, 11, 16², 21; 2:7, 16, 18; 3:2², 4², 5, 12, 13, 15, 17
Granville Sharp Construction, 2 Pt 1:3; 2:10a, 20; 3:2, 18

hapax legomenon, 2 Pt 1:1, 9, 15², 17², 19², 20; 2:1², 3², 4, 6, 8², 10a, 10b, 13, 14, 16², 17, 18, 22⁴; 3:3, 6, 9, 10², 12, 14, 16³, 17
haplography, Jd 22; 2 Pt 3:8
hendiadys, 2 Pt 1:16

idiom, Jd 16; 2 Pt 1:13; 2:8, 12, 15; 3:18
ἴδιος (reflexive), 2 Pt 3:16
ἰδού, Jd 14
imperative mood, Jd 21, 22, 23²; 2 Pt 1:10; 3:8, 18
imperfect tense, Jd 18; 2 Pt 2:21

impersonal expression, 2 Pt 3:5
implied verb, Jd 11
improper preposition, Jd 16, 24
ἵνα (purpose), 2 Pt 1:4; 3:17
inclusio, Jd 1; 2 Pt 1:11; 2:1; 3:7, 13
infinitive (complementary), Jd 5, 9, 24^2; 2 Pt 1:10, 12, 13, 15^2; 2:9; 3:9, 11
infinitive (epexegetical), Jd 3^2
infinitive (indirect discourse), Jd 3
infinitive (purpose), Jd 15^2; 2 Pt 3:2
infinitive (subject), 2 Pt 2:21^2
interjection, Jd 10

καί, Jd 22, 25; 2 Pt 1:19; 2:2, 3; 3:3, 5
καί (adverbial), Jd 23; 2 Pt 2:1^2, 2, 12
καί ... καί, 2 Pt 3:18
καίπερ (concessive conjunction), 2 Pt 1:12
καθώς (comparative), 2 Pt 1:14; 3:15
κατά (opposition), Jd 15^2; 2 Pt 2:11
κατά (standard), Jd 16, 18; 2 Pt 3:3, 13, 15

left-dislocation, Jd 10; 2 Pt 3:6

μέλλω (periphrastic future), 2 Pt 1:12
μέν, Jd 22
μετά (temporal), 2 Pt 1:15
middle voice, 2 Pt 2:19, 22; 3:4

nominal clause, 2 Pt 2:10b
nominative absolute, Jd 1; 2 Pt 1:1, 8; 2:19, 22^2
nominative in apposition, Jd 1, 4, 9, 12^5, 13^2, 14, 16, 19; 2 Pt 1:1^2, 17; 2:10b; 3:15
nominative of address, Jd 3
nominative of exclamation, 2 Pt 2:10b, 14
nominative subject, Jd 2, 4, 5, 7, 8, 9^2, 10^2, 12, 13, 14^2, 15, 16^3, 17, 18, 19, 20, 25^4; 2 Pt 1:2, 8, 9, 11, 14^2, 17, 18, 19^2, 20, 21^2; 2:1^2, 2, 3^2, 4, 8, 9, 11, 12, 15, 16, 17, 19, 20, 22; 3:4^3, 5^3, 7, 8, 9^2, 10^4, 12, 13, 15, 16^3, 17
nominative subject of an implied verb, 2 Pt 2:11; 3:10, 18
nominative subject of a verbless equative clause, 2 Pt 2:17; 3:8^2
νῦν, 2 Pt 3:7

object-complement double accusative, Jd 24^2; 2 Pt 1:8^2, 10, 13, 19; 2:6, 13; 3:15
ὀπίσω (spatial preposition), 2 Pt 2:10a
ὅπου (causal), 2 Pt 2:11
ὅπου (expressing a premise), 2 Pt 2:11
optative mood (wish, prayer, or blessing), Jd 2, 9, 25; 2 Pt 1:2
ὅς, Jd 22, 23^2
ὅσος (correlative adjective), Jd 10
ὅτι (causal), Jd 11
ὅτι (clausal complement), Jd 5; 2 Pt 1:14
ὅτι (clausal complement; indirect discourse with a verb of cognition), Jd 18
ὅτι (epexegetical), Jd 18; 2 Pt 1:20; 3:3, 5, 8
οὐ (negating participle), 2 Pt 1:16

Grammar Index

οὗτος (demonstrive pronoun, resumptive), Jd 10, 16, 19; 2 Pt 2:17
οὕτως (adverb of manner), 2 Pt 1:11; 3:4, 11

πάλαι, Jd 4
παρά (source), 2 Pt 1:17; 2:11
παρά (viewpoint), 2 Pt 3:8
parataxis, 2 Pt 3:9
part-whole figure of speech, Jd 16
participle (adverbial), Jd 12
participle (attributive), Jd 1, 3, 4³, 5, 6², 7², 8, 12², 13, 16, 17, 18, 22, 23; 2 Pt 1:12, 16, 18, 19; 2:1, 4, 7, 9, 11², 13, 14², 17, 21, 22²; 3:2, 3, 4, 15
participle (attendant circumstance), Jd 9, 16, 20²; 2 Pt 2:1, 15, 16, 19; 3:7, 12²
participle (causal), 2 Pt 1:9, 14, 20; 2:15, 20; 3:9, 14, 17
participle (complementary), 2 Pt 2:9; 3:14
participle (concessive), 2 Pt 1:12²; 2:1, 11
participle (condition), 2 Pt 1:8², 10, 19
participle (imperatival), 2 Pt 3:3
participle (manner), Jd 14; 2 Pt 2:4; 3:3, 4, 5
participle (means), Jd 7, 20², 23²; 2 Pt 1:5, 10, 16², 19; 2:4, 6, 15, 18; 3:6, 12²
participle (periphrastic), 2 Pt 3:5, 7²
participle (predicate), 2 Pt 1:9², 19; 2:13², 14³, 15
participle (purpose), Jd 3

participle (result), 2 Pt 2:1², 6
participle (substantival), Jd 5, 12², 19², 24; 2 Pt 1:1, 3; 2:4, 6, 10a², 18², 21; 3:12²
participle (supplementary), 2 Pt 1:19; 2:10b
participle (temporal), Jd 3, 5, 21; 2 Pt 1:4, 17, 18, 21; 2:5, 8, 10b, 13², 20, 21; 3:14, 16
πᾶς, position of, Jd 15, 25²
πᾶς (class as a whole), 2 Pt 1:20
πᾶς (distributive), 2 Pt 1:20
passive voice, 2 Pt 1:2; 2:2, 19
perfect tense, Jd 6, 10; 2 Pt 2:20; 3:7
περί (reference), Jd 3, 15²; 2 Pt 1:12; 3:16
περί (spatial), Jd 7
peroratio, Jd 24
pleonastic, 2 Pt 2:17; 3:3
pluperfect tense (periphrastic), 2 Pt 3:5
polyptoton, 2 Pt 2:10b
ποτέ, 2 Pt 1:10
ποῦ, 2 Pt 3:4
predicate adjective, 2 Pt 1:9, 14; 2:20, 21; 3:16
predicate interogative adverb, 2 Pt 3:4
predicate nominative, Jd 12², 16; 2 Pt 1:16, 17; 2:11, 19
predicate nominative of a verbless equative clause, 2 Pt 2:13², 14, 17²
prepositional phrase (adverbial), Jd 24
present tense, 2 Pt 2:20; 3:4
πρό (temporal), Jd 25
πρός (reference), 2 Pt 1:3
πρός (result), 2 Pt 3:16

protasis, 2 Pt 2:4, 5
πρῶτος (adverbial), 2 Pt 1:20

relative clause, Jd 13, 15²; 2 Pt 1:3, 9, 17; 3:6, 10, 16
right-dislocation, Jd 15

Semitic influence (Semitism), Jd 11³, 15, 16, 21, 24, 25; 2 Pt 1:20; 2:3, 9, 10a, 14, 15; 3:3², 8, 10
subject-complement double nominative, 2 Pt 3:14
subjunctive mood (in emphatic negation), 2 Pt 1:10
subjunctive mood (in ἵνα purpose clause), 2 Pt 3:17
subjunctive mood (in indefinite temporal clause), 2 Pt 1:19²
σύν (association), 2 Pt 1:18
superlative, Jd 20; 2 Pt 1:4

tautology, 2 Pt 2:10b
τε *solitarium*, Jd 6
τοιόσδε (demonstrative adjective), 2 Pt 1:17

τότε, 2 Pt 3:6
τοῦτος (demonstrative pronoun), 2 Pt 3:3
τοῦτος (resumptive pronoun), Jd 10

ὑπό (spatial), Jd 6
ὑπό (ultimate agency), Jd 12, 17; 2 Pt 1:17, 21; 2:7, 17; 3:2

vocative, 2 Pt 1:10; 3:1, 14, 17
vocative in apposition, Jd 17, 20; 2 Pt 3:8

word play, Jd 6
ὡς (adjectival in predicate position), 2 Pt 3:8
ὡς (clausal complement), Jd 7; 2 Pt 1:3
ὡς (comparative), 2 Pt 1:19; 2:12; 3:9, 10, 16
ὡς (temporal), 2 Pt 3:8

AUTHOR INDEX

Abbott, xxi
Aland, xvi

Bakker, xii
Bauckham, xxi, 11, 13, 44, 45
BDAG, xv, 6, 8, 9, 11, 14, 15, 16, 18, 19, 22, 23, 25, 26, 27, 28, 30, 31, 33, 34, 35, 38, 41, 43, 44, 45, 46, 47, 48, 50, 51, 52, 53, 54, 55, 56, 57, 58, 59, 61, 62, 65, 66, 67, 69, 70, 71, 72, 73, 74, 75, 76, 77, 78, 79, 80, 81, 82, 83, 84, 85, 86, 87, 88, 89, 90, 91, 92, 94, 96, 97, 98, 99, 101, 102, 103, 104, 106, 107, 108, 110, 111, 112
BDF, xv, 5, 6, 11, 12, 15, 16, 18, 22, 23, 24, 25, 27, 28, 30, 33, 35, 38, 41, 42, 45, 46, 47, 49, 53, 55, 56, 57, 58, 59, 60, 61, 62, 63, 64, 66, 67, 68, 69, 70, 71, 72, 73, 77, 82, 84, 85, 86, 87, 88, 89, 90, 91, 92, 93, 94, 95, 96, 97, 101, 103, 104, 105, 107, 108, 109, 110, 111, 112
Bovon, 17
Büchsel, 36
Bultmann, 33, 41

Caragounis, xii
Conrad, xii, xiii
Culy, vii, 8, 11, 54, 59, 60, 70, 106, 108
Culy and Parsons, 11, 60

Davids, xix, xx, 6, 49, 57, 104
Delling, 40, 104

Friberg, xv, 5, 9, 10, 11, 15, 21, 23, 24, 28, 30, 35, 39, 40, 43, 47, 49, 50, 53, 54, 55, 68, 71, 73, 82, 84, 86, 91, 92, 95, 98, 104, 105, 108, 110

Green, 73

Hauck, 39
Heiser, 22

Kraus, xxi, 2

Landon, xix
Levinsohn, 9
Lukaszewski, xv

Marshall, 17
Metzger, 78, 80, 81, 104, 105, 112
MHT, xvi, xx, xxi, 23, 25, 26, 28,

30, 34, 35, 38, 40, 42, 45, 46, 47, 49, 53, 55, 56, 57, 58, 59, 60, 61, 62, 67, 68, 69, 70, 71, 72, 73, 74, 75, 76, 77, 82, 84, 87, 88, 89, 90, 91, 92, 93, 94, 95, 96, 97, 98, 99, 100, 102, 103, 104, 105, 107, 108, 110
Michel, 33
Miller, xv
Mounce, 59

Parsons, 59
Penner, 22
Pennington, xii, xiii
Porter, 15, 53, 59, 76, 89

Reese, 5
Robertson, xii, 35
Runge, 7, 13, 115

Schmidt, 31
Schweizer, 31
Stählin, 38

Taylor, xii, xiii
Towner, 2
Turner, xx, xxi, 25

Wallace, xi, xvi, 19, 27, 33, 34, 38, 40, 42, 45, 49, 53, 57, 59, 60, 62, 63, 65, 66, 67, 68, 72, 74, 76, 80, 83, 91, 94, 96, 97, 98, 99, 107, 108, 109, 112, 114
Watson, xix, xxi

Young, 114

Zerwick, xvi, 44, 49

www.ingramcontent.com/pod-product-compliance
Lightning Source LLC
Chambersburg PA
CBHW030556230426
43661CB00054B/2161